W9-BRN-731

Northern Lights
Going to the Sources

Stephen Sandell

Minnesota Historical Society Press

St. Paul

1989

Copy and production editor: Ellen B. Green
Pilot design: Monica Little
Final design and layout: Thomas McGregor
Typesetting and keyline: Northwestern Printcrafters, Inc.
Printing: Bolger Publications, Inc.
Research assistants: Andrea Lanoux
                    Ken Simon
                    Deborah Swanson
                    David Wiggins
Project interns: Kristi Anderson
                    Cassandra Wensel

Illustration credits appear on page 215.

© 1989 by Minnesota Historical Society. All rights reserved

Book ISBN: 0-87351-242-1   Set ISBN: 0-87351-243-X

Manufactured in the United States of America

Northern Lights
Going to the Sources

Contents

Unit I
A Place of Many Faces

Unit II
Changing Worlds

Preface

Next time you go to a play, ask for a seat behind the scenes. You will have an unusual view of the stage. You may miss some of what the audience sees. You may not hear every speech spoken by each actor. Instead, you will be interrupted by a manager giving directions to the stage crew. You may see the director coaching a performer. You may even hear the author decide to change a character's lines. You will see all the ingredients of the production prepared for the audience.

Reading this book is like going to a play and sitting behind the scenes. It is an unusual way to study history. The stories in this book are often interrupted while you search for more information about what happened next. You will struggle to find answers about the past from contradictory sources or from too little information. You will discover that events are seldom the result of a single cause. You will even be asked to write some history yourself.

While you study history from behind the scenes, you may learn some things hidden from other readers. You will learn that history has an imperfect memory. You will learn that events, people, and ideas are often forgotten or misunderstood as times change. You will discover that history has its own personality, with fascinating characteristics that make it different from every other subject you study.

Together with *The Story of Minnesota's Past*, and a teacher's edition, *Going to the Sources* is part of the *Northern Lights* curriculum of Minnesota history.

Support and encouragement for *Northern Lights* has come from teachers, students, scholars, librarians, and others interested in Minnesota history. Many of them offered their time, suggestions, and criticism to strengthen this project. A grant from the legislature and technical assistance from the Minnesota Department of Education made it possible to test and evaluate *Northern Lights* in classrooms throughout the state. A generous loan and grant from the Blandin Foundation of Grand Rapids, Minnesota, supported the research, writing, and publication of the books.

Members of the Minnesota Historical Society's Education Department read drafts of the manuscript and offered advice and ideas for improvement. Rhoda Gilman, author of *The Story of Minnesota's Past*, Stephen Sandell, author of *Going to the Sources*, and Maureen Otwell of the Minnesota Historical Society have been responsible for the development and organization of the curriculum. *Going to the Sources* owes a particular debt to researchers Andrea Lanoux, Ken Simon, Deborah Swanson, and David Wiggins who provided ideas, insight, and hard work. Ellen Green of E. B. Green Editorial served as editor and production coordinator; Monica Little of Little & Company and Thomas McGregor of McGregor Design were the designers.

This volume is dedicated to the people who encouraged these ideas, those who kept me at it to the end, and to the legacy of James Blaine Hedges, a great teacher.

Minnesota became a state in 1858. From 1849 to 1858 Minnesota Territory included the area called Dacotah. This map was made in 1860.

This photograph was made in 1979 from images recorded by a special camera carried on a satellite, 570 miles above the earth. The camera recorded light reflected from earth. Each speck of light was turned into a computer code and beamed to earth where it was recorded on computer tape.

A computer system turned the code into a laser signal that burned an image onto a piece of film. The film was developed and printed as a photograph.

Photographs like these are used to study the effects of events like fires and floods, or human activity like farming and pollution, on our natural resources.

This photograph is a mosaic—an image made from many smaller snapshots taken from space.

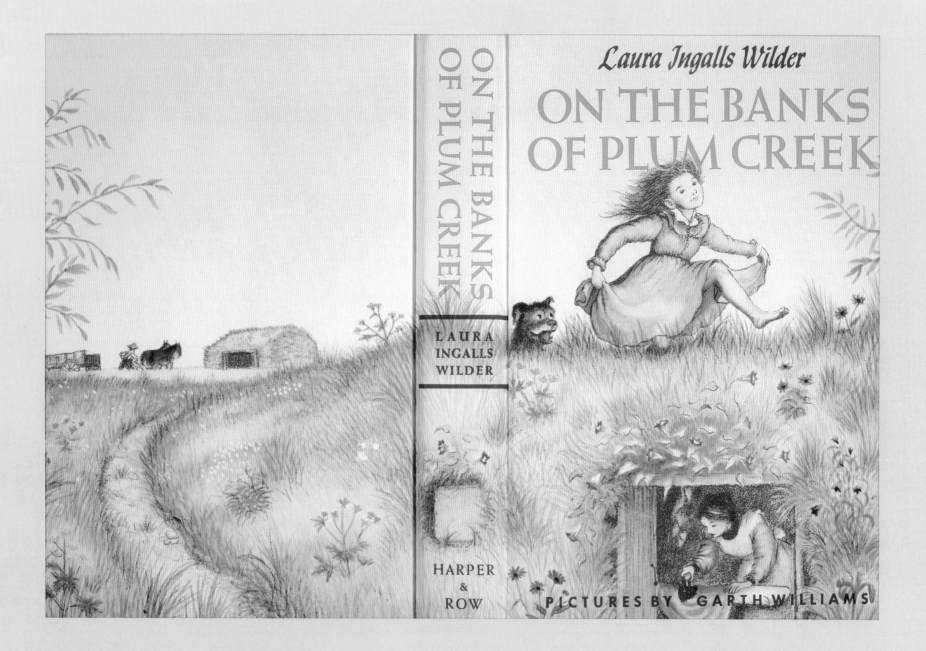

Activity 1
Questions, Evidence, and Information

Laura Ingalls arrived in Minnesota on a covered wagon pulled by two horses. She was nine years old. Her parents were farmers. They had lived in Wisconsin, Missouri, and Indian Territory before coming to Minnesota.

Laura's family settled along Plum Creek near a small town called Walnut Grove. They traded their wagon cover and horses for a house dug out of the banks along the creek. That was in 1876, more than a hundred years ago.

The family lived along Plum Creek for two years before deciding to move again. They went first to Iowa, then back to Walnut Grove, and finally to South Dakota.

When Laura Ingalls was older, she wrote books about her childhood. *Little House on the Prairie, On the Banks of Plum Creek,* and *The Long Winter* are some of the books she wrote. In 1943, an artist named Garth Williams was asked to draw pictures for Laura's books. He agreed to work on the project.

The artist wanted to make sure his drawings were accurate. He needed to know what it was like to live in the woods, on the prairie, and in a small town during the 1870s. He started by asking questions and looking for historical evidence.

Historical evidence is anything that provides information about the past. Newspapers, letters, diaries, photographs, and maps may be evidence. Even a building, a tool, or a piece of clothing can provide information.

Before drawing this picture, artist Garth Williams found the spot along Plum Creek near where the Ingalls family lived. He studied Laura's description of the house she remembered: All around the door green vines were growing out of the grassy bank. The dugout home was one room. The earth walls were smoothed and whitewashed. The earth floor was smooth and hard. Grass grew on the roof and waved in the wind, just like all the grass along the creek bank.

Historians study evidence to learn about the past. They use newspapers, letters, maps, tools, and machinery to learn about events, people, and ideas. What evidence did Garth Williams need to draw this picture?

Garth Williams wrote a story about what he learned by living with his family on a farm: "We had neither telephone nor electricity. Our water came down from a crystal-clear spring in the woods. Our only mechanical convenience was a hand-pump in the kitchen, located in a lean-to with a very leaky roof."

Sometimes evidence is easy to find. Other times the search is difficult and takes a long time, even years. Garth Williams was lucky. He had a chance to talk with Laura in person at her home. "She took us into the house and we looked at all her old family photographs. She told us about the people and just where to find Plum Creek and other places mentioned in the books."

Garth Williams traveled to some of the places Laura had lived with her family. He tried to imagine himself in a covered wagon creeping slowly across the prairie.

When he arrived in Walnut Grove, he stopped at the newspaper office and talked with the editor. They looked for evidence of the Ingalls family in old newspapers. They found pictures of the town and the people. They even found Pa Ingalls's name in one issue.

Garth asked for directions to the site of the Ingalls home on Plum Creek. He followed the di-

Garth Williams learned how white settlers built their houses and other farm buildings on the prairie. The walls of the stable were of sod. The roof was willow boughs and hay, with sod laid over it. The roof was so low that Pa's head touched it when he stood up straight. For the milk cow, Pa traded a day's work with a farmer who needed help haying and harvesting. Garth Williams needed information about clothing and even kitchen utensils to draw this scene accurately.

rections along a muddy path to the creek. He walked along the stream for a long time. "I was just about to give up when ahead of me I saw exactly what I was looking for, a hollow in the east bank of Plum Creek. The scene fit Laura's description perfectly."

Garth Williams needed to know about the things Laura's family used on the farm and in their home. He visited museums to look at clothing and farm equipment used in the 1870s. In one museum he found a jug with the name Ingalls on it.

Pictures by Garth Williams appear in each of Laura's books. They help to tell the stories Laura remembered. The evidence Williams found—the old farm, the newspaper, photographs, the talk with Laura, and the descriptions in her books—provided information to help make his drawings as accurate as possible.

Laura's family moved from the dugout into a home made of lumber. Garth Williams searched for information before drawing this picture. Where do you think he looked? Carrie, Mary, and Laura Ingalls are at right.

Collecting Evidence

About the time Laura Ingalls began writing, a young man named Way Quah Gishig was growing up in northern Minnesota. He was an Ojibway Indian.

Way Quah and his family lived on the White Earth Reservation, near the town of Bagley. His mother spoke only Ojibway. Way Quah and his sisters learned English at a boarding school in South Dakota. At school, Way Quah was called John Rogers. At home he used his Ojibway name.

Way Quah wrote a book about his childhood, too. His book is called *Red World and White*. It describes his days at boarding school and many things he learned from his family and from nature.

Way Quah Gishig did not illustrate his book. That's a job for you. Search for information in the following pieces of evidence. Then describe the past, as Garth Williams did, in pictures. If you do a good job of collecting and studying evidence, what you learn will help tell a story.

Locate White Earth Reservation on a map of Minnesota. Way Quah wrote about the day in 1906 when he came home from boarding school. He arrived on a train with his two sisters, Min di and Bishiu.

From *Red World and White* by John Rogers, first published in 1957 as *A Chippewa Speaks:*

Mahnomen was a new town when Way Quah arrived on the train from boarding school in 1906.

We got off the puffing, snorting train at Mahnomen, Minnesota. A man named John Carr met us. He put us in his wagon.

We stopped briefly at the town of Beaulieu, where we got out and stretched our legs and had lunch. When we started out again, we came into wooded places, where trees seemed to tower upward to the sky and cast deep dark shadows on the fallen leaves encircling them.

Finally Min di turned and exclaimed, "Look, Way Quah!" She pointed toward the north. There in the distance I saw the sparkle of water and the ripple of waves as the sun was reflected back through the trees. This I knew was home!

The first night Way Quah spent talking with his mother and sisters around the wigwam fire. "Mother promised to teach me the ways of the forest, rivers, and lakes," he wrote.

Way Quah lived with his mother and three sisters in their wigwam at White Earth. He learned from his mother how to collect food, trap animals, and help provide for his family. Their wigwam was different from the dugout home where Laura Ingalls lived. This is the way he remembered it:

Mother's wigwam was about the size of a large room in a white man's dwelling. In the center was a fireplace, and above in the middle of the roof was an opening for light and for the smoke to escape. Suspended from a framework over the fire were two kettles almost full of water.

On one side of this large room I saw a bedframe made of poles. Over these were laid boughs to make a smooth, springly couch about the size of a double bed. The bedding consisted of deer pelts and, when not in use, could be folded back to the wall and serve as a back-rest.

Along the east wall was mother's workshop, and opposite the door the kitchen equipment was kept. On the west side was a place for the man's workshop. Over at the opposite wall was the pit used for storing and the

A traditional Ojibway home similar to Way Quah's wigwam

Residents of White Earth Reservation, about 1900. What does this photo tell you about the people who lived there?

wood pile. *The storage pit was a hole dug in the ground, and this was overlaid with hay, on top of which was some birch bark. Here were potatoes, carrots, corn, onions, and any canned or dried fruits that had accumulated from the gather of fruits and berries.*

By 1910 most Ojibway families at White Earth chose to live in homes built of lumber:

The time came when we moved into our new home. How different it was from the one-room wigwam to which we had been accustomed. Despite the fact that this new place was such a departure from the ways of the native Indian life, we all took great pride in fixing it up.

It was a log cabin and gave out a smell of pine and birch. Tall trees towered around the house and there were the merry chirps of birds and the call of wild life, just as it had been before. All that we had given up really was our wigwam with its crude beds and the firepit in the center of the one room.

Now we had three rooms—two of them bedrooms. The other was very large and was used as a combined kitchen and living room. The roof was thatched. This, together with the log structure, blended into the surrounding forest so naturally that even an Indian would hardly have found his way to the little clearing without knowing its exact location.

Our nearest neighbor was half a day's walk through heavy growth of trees and brush. The only trail was that of the wolf, the deer, or the bear.

The bark baskets above are similar to those used by Way Quah's mother. Compare the Mille Lacs Ojibway home at right with Way Quah's description of his mother's wigwam.

Tepee interior Lake Mille Lacs

Drawing from Information

The photographs, maps, and description of Way Quah's home are similar to the evidence Garth Williams found. They provide information for drawing pictures of events, people, and places in Way Quah's life.

Choose a scene from Way Quah's life to illustrate. Draw the town of Mahnomen, or the wigwam Way Quah described. Draw the tools and equipment found in a wigwam, the new cabin at White Earth, or whatever you like.

When you finish, write a caption about your drawing. Compare your drawing to others in class. Did you include the same information? Did you include things that Way Quah didn't mention? Did you make up anything? Do you think your drawing is accurate?

Don't worry if you don't seem to know enough about the places and the times to get everything right. Garth Williams felt that way, too. Even with all the information he collected, his drawings are not always accurate. There were some things he left out of his drawings and other things he just didn't know.

We will never be able to learn everything about the past or to draw pictures with everything just the way it was. The best you can do is search hard for evidence, collect information, and tell the story as accurately as possible.

Changes in traditional Ojibway life are easy to see in this photograph taken at White Earth Reservation. The small structures near the front are graves.

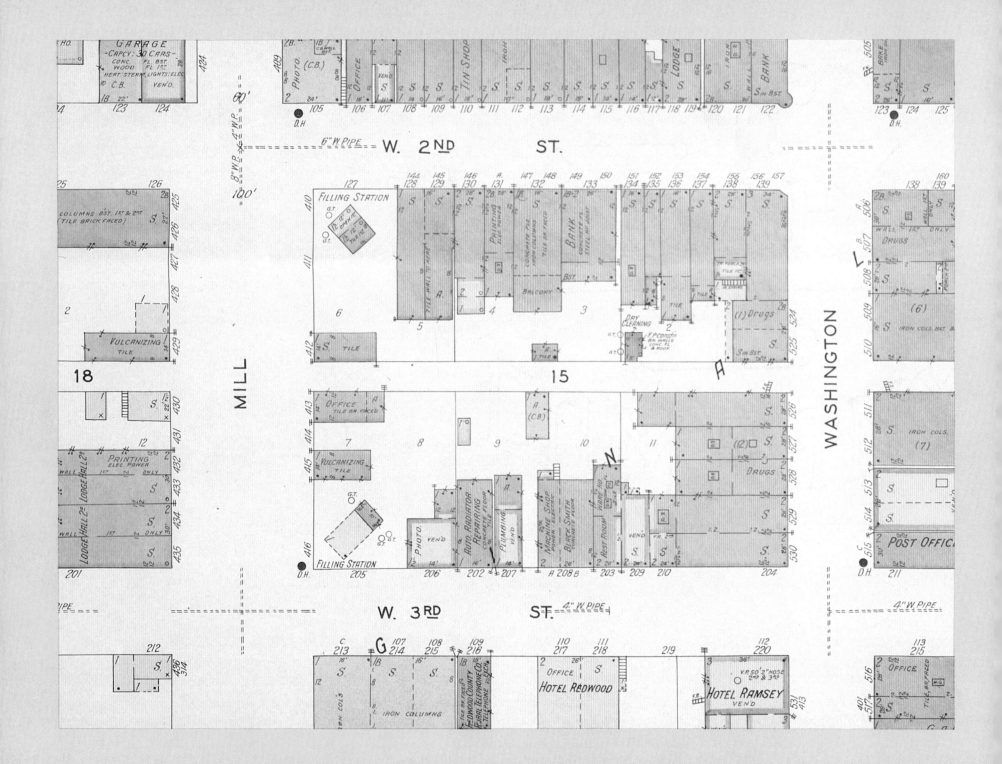

Activity 2
What Do You See on a Map?

Before people drew maps on paper, they used words to describe places and distances. They named landmarks like hills, lakes, and trees to direct others from one place to another. They told distance by the time it took to get there.

When people began drawing maps, they used symbols for places and landmarks. An X or a small circle showed where someone lived or hunted. A long line indicated a great distance. A wiggly line represented a river or a stream. When people printed maps on paper, they used other symbols and color to give information about location and distance.

The more people traveled, the more information they collected about places and distances. They learned to draw more accurate maps to show the relationship of one place to another. They drew road maps and maps showing the boundaries between cities or territories. Their maps indicated mountains, rivers, bridges, buildings, and settlements of people.

People who draw maps collect large amounts of information before they begin their work. They can't use all the information in a single map. It's their job to select just the right information, then get it down in a way that helps you understand and use it. A map with everything we know about a place would be very difficult to draw or to read.

Maps are important evidence for historians. They can provide information about the location of events and the way things change over time.

People who study geography use maps, too. They use maps to determine the location of places and events. They learn what it is that makes one place different from all others. They use maps to study the relationships between one place and another. They also study maps to learn how people have lived in different places around the world.

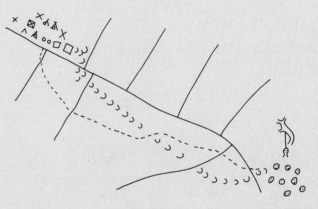

This map represents the path a Hidatsa man took along the Missouri River to a Dakota camp.

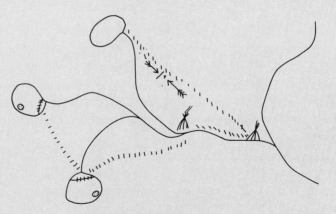

Originally drawn on birch bark, this map shows the route two Indian men took while trapping beaver. Can you pick out the campsites and beaver dams?

This detail from a map of Redwood Falls, 1928, shows only a small part of town. Buildings made of wood are yellow. Brick buildings are pink. Stone buildings are blue.

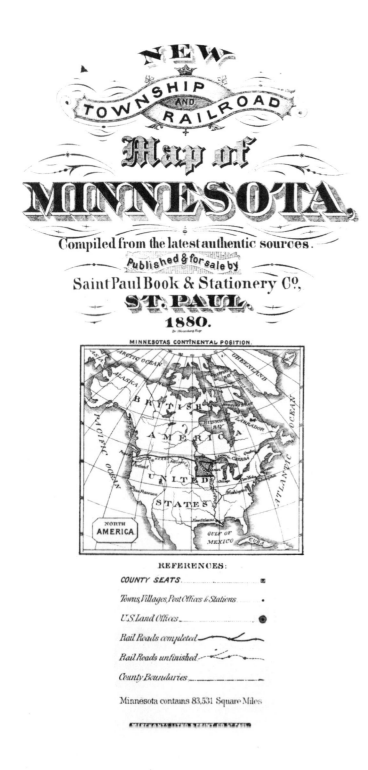

NEW TOWNSHIP AND RAILROAD Map of MINNESOTA.

Compiled from the latest authentic sources.

Published & for sale by

Saint Paul Book & Stationery Co,

ST. PAUL.

1880.

MINNESOTAS CONTINENTAL POSITION.

NORTH AMERICA

REFERENCES:

COUNTY SEATS

Towns, Villages, Post Offices & Stations

U.S Land Offices

Rail Roads completed

Rail Roads unfinished

County Boundaries

Minnesota contains 83,531 Square Miles

Geographers and historians aren't the only ones who use maps. Most of us use maps to get from one place to another, to find a certain store in the shopping center, to learn the distance from one freeway exit to another, to locate the deepest spot in the lake, or to find a seat at a concert or a game.

Just like a book, most maps have guides for people who want to use them. Instead of a table of contents or an index, however, maps have TOADS.

TOADS is shorthand for the information that you can find on most maps. Each letter of the word stands for a piece of information that helps a historian, a geographer, or you to use the map.

The TOADS are usually found together in a corner of the map called the key (or legend).

Maps are a little like the pictures in a family photo album.

TOADS help you find your way around a map. This is how they are used:

T: Every map has a title.

O: Most maps have a symbol to indicate the direction of north, south, east, and west. Some maps have an arrow showing "You are here." That is called orientation. It helps you get started in the right direction.

A: The author is the person or group of people who drew the map.

D: Look for a date on your map. It tells you when the map was made.

S: Pay attention to the scale of your map. This indicates how many miles or feet are represented by an inch on the map. An inch on one map may represent just a few feet. On another, it may represent a hundred miles.

Not all maps include each of the TOADS. Study each of these map keys to see what information is missing.

Each picture in the album tells you something about the family. From one photo you can tell what kind of car they once drove. From another, you can learn what their house looked like. Photos taken at different times show changes in the way people looked or in the clothes they wore. It takes more than one photograph to learn very much about a family.

Maps work the same way. The more maps you have to study, the more you can learn. That's why historians and geographers use several maps to study places and events.

Some mapmakers leave the orientation symbol off their maps. No compass indicates north, south, east, or west for the maps on these pages. When that happens, you can assume north is at the top of the map. Check the maps in your classroom. Are each of the TOADS included?

A Spot on the Map

THE REDWOOD GAZETTE

PUBLISHED TO PROMOTE THE BEST INTERESTS OF REDWOOD FALLS AND REDWOOD COUNTY

REDWOOD FALLS, MINNESOTA, WEDNESDAY, SEPT. 13, 1916.

Bess Wilson became owner and editor of the Redwood Gazette *in 1916.*

The city of Redwood Falls is in southwestern Minnesota, near the northern border of Redwood County and close to the Minnesota River. Find it on the state map on page 25.

Use the map's scale to tell how far it is from Redwood Falls north to Willmar, east to Shakopee, south to Windom, and west to Marshall. Find the Redwood River running through town and into the larger Minnesota River about a mile north.

Maps provide more information than just distance and direction. If you study maps closely, you can learn the geography and some of the history of a city like Redwood Falls.

You could put yourself in the place of Bess Wilson, who moved to Redwood Falls with her husband and two children in 1911. She started working for the town newspaper, the *Redwood Gazette,* in 1913. Three years later she became its owner and editor. Until

The Redwood River meets the Minnesota River just north of Redwood Falls.

she sold the paper and moved to Minneapolis in 1927, Bess Wilson wrote many of the stories in the *Redwood Gazette*. Almost everyone in town knew her.

The *Gazette* office was on the south side of West 2nd Street, in the middle of the block, between Washington and Mill avenues. When Bess Wilson stood on the sidewalk in front of her office, she could look west toward Mill Avenue and see the Redwood River. When she looked east, toward Washington Avenue, she could see the dome and steeple of the county courthouse two blocks away.

Imagine that it is May 6, 1926, and that you are Bess Wilson. After working all day on the paper, you have decided to write a letter to a friend in your hometown of St. Charles, Minnesota. Tell your friend about Redwood Falls—what it looks like, what it is like to live there, and what people do there.

Find this building on the map of Redwood Falls, page 18. What streets are on each side of it? When do you think the photo was taken? The cars are one clue. The attendant is pumping gas by hand.

Looking east on 3rd Street in Redwood Falls, 1915. The county courthouse is in the distance.

Picture a Place

How can you describe a place that you haven't seen, and that no longer looks as it did more than 60 years ago? Geographers and historians often collect information about places present and past by asking questions and searching maps.

Take a look at the four maps in this chapter. The state and county maps are on page 25. A map of Redwood Falls is on this page. Finally, a map of the neighborhood in downtown Redwood Falls is on page 18.

You will see right away that each map has a different scale. Though they all include Redwood Falls, each one provides different information about it. The state and county maps show the relationship of Redwood Falls to other towns in the region. They provide few details about the people and places in town. The town and neighborhood maps offer a close look at the streets and buildings where people live and work. They don't tell you about the area outside the city limits.

Now use the maps to answer the following questions. Study the maps—one by one—and write down the information you learn about Redwood Falls in 1926.

1. What does the town look like? (Are there rivers, mountains, lakes, or forests in the area? Is Redwood Falls a big city or a small town? Is it in an area of farms, prairie, or forests?)

The State Bank of Redwood Falls was on the corner of Washington Avenue and 2nd Street. A barbershop was in the basement, and a drugstore was next door. Locate the bank on this town map of Redwood Falls. The maps at right, along with the pictures on pages 22 and 23, give an idea of what the town looked like.

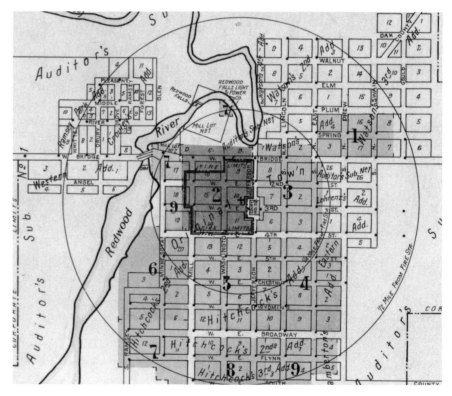

The town of Redwood Falls, about 1925

2. How do people use the town? (Do people live and work here? Does the town have a special use like business, industry, housing, religion, sports, government, or education? Can you tell whether the town has changed much over time?)

3. What happens in Redwood Falls that might be important to people living somewhere else? (Do people come here for church, school, government, fun, or business?)

4. How do people, information, and materials travel to and from Redwood Falls? (Do they use automobiles and trucks, airplanes, trains, small boats, or large ships? Is there evidence of electricity for telephones, radio, or television?)

By now you know the town almost as well as Bess Wilson and you can write the letter to your hometown friend. Begin with the date May 6, 1926.

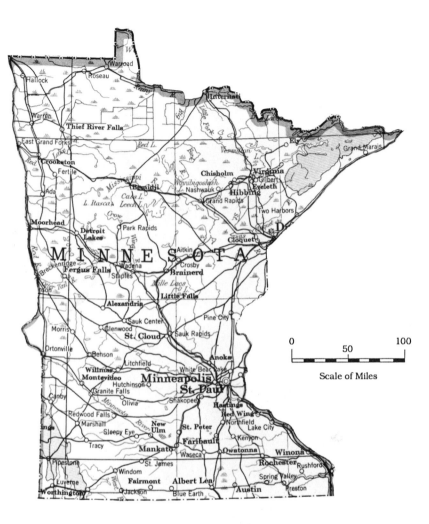

Railroad lines are drawn on the map of Redwood County at left, but highways are not. The state map above shows major highways in 1948.

Activity 3
Moving a Town

When Frank Hibbing began to prospect for iron ore in northern Minnesota in 1892, he used a map. It helped him find his way north from Duluth to the place where he expected to find ore. The map showed landmarks like roads, lakes, and the edge of the forest.

The location he chose to look for iron ore was about 75 miles north of Duluth and about 100 miles south of Canada. He knew where to look and was lucky enough to find the ore. He marked the spot on his map and traveled back to Duluth, where he claimed the land for a mine and a townsite.

Hibbing and his partner hired men and equipment to dig for ore. Their business grew and their settlement grew, too. By June 1893, over 300 people lived there. They held an election and voted to call their town the Village of Hibbing.

By 1910 Hibbing was no longer a small settlement of prospectors. Almost 9,000 people lived in town. There were schools, churches, family homes, and boardinghouses. There was a city hall and there were businesses along the main street. Roads and railroads were built through town.

The mines grew bigger and faster than anyone expected. The companies that owned them grew wealthy and powerful. Men and machines stripped away the earth and dug for iron ore at the edge of town. In 1919, Hibbing was surrounded on the north, east, and west by mines. The homes and stores, schools and churches, hotels and other buildings that were important to everyday life stood in the way of the mines. They would all have to move if the mines were to grow.

Miners and steam shovels dug for valuable iron ore. Before long, the mines reached the edge of town. The mining companies needed the land on which employees' homes were built. The town moved while the mines grew.

The colors and shapes in this painting by Cameron Booth give you a feeling of the busy, noisy, growing industry of iron mining in northern Minnesota. Booth made this painting in 1937 and called it Hibbing Mine. Once Booth said his paintings were like music without words. Do you think that's a good way to describe this one?

By summer of 1919, the mining companies had already moved some buildings. The newspaper editor wrote: "This land is presumed to have one of the largest deposits of iron ore in the area. The steamshovels are crowding closer upon the village every year. The next few years will surely see great changes in Hibbing."

Some people in Hibbing didn't want to move. They asked the government to stop the whole thing, but that didn't work. Most people agreed with the newspaper that: "Business must proceed even if some people are disturbed. The world has to move."

At first a few small buildings at the edge of town were moved south, away from the mines. But it was clear that more of the town would follow. The iron ore underneath was too valuable for the town to stand in the way.

Movers lifted the buildings one by one off their foundations and onto rollers. They wrapped some with steel cables and moved them almost two miles south. Steam engines that had been used to haul logs out of the forest pulled the buildings.

On July 15, 1919, a reporter wrote about the move in the *Hibbing Daily Tribune:* "A new town is rapidly springing up. The Oliver Iron Mining Company has moved most of the houses on Cedar and Center streets lying between 1st and 2nd avenues out to their new townsite. Many other buildings

Hibbing businesses grew quickly when iron was discovered. By 1910, when this picture was taken, the town's main street was busy every day. The mining companies and workers needed supplies, equipment, and services. All this had to go to make room for the growing mines.

are being moved from various locations in the old Hibbing, and a house can be seen moving rapidly down 1st Avenue almost every day.

"The town is on the move, and it keeps residents and business-men guessing as to just how much of it will move and what will be-come of the rest of it. It is a big operation and cannot be done all at once. But it is certain that the Oliver Iron Mining Company will need the ore on the townsite."

Buildings from Hibbing being moved to their new sites. The move continued from 1919 to the 1950s.

This moving crew stopped for a photograph in front of the Colonia Hotel. The building was lifted onto a platform with wheels and pulled by a steam tractor to its new site.

Get Out of the Way!

Frank Dear and his family were among the first to move. They lived on the north side of town, just two blocks from the mines. Their address was 202 Center Street. From the porch on the second floor of their house, they could see machinery stripping the earth away at the edge of town.

In September 1919, arrangements were made to move the Dears' house. A crew of movers used heavy equipment to lift the house off its foundation and onto a sled of huge timbers and solid steel wheels. They attached the house and sled to a steam-powered tractor.

On September 16, the tractor and house began moving to the new townsite. The tractor coughed smoke and steam. The wheels of the sled moved and the wooden house creaked. It rocked with each bump in the road. The crew was careful with the load. They knew that any mistake could cause a serious accident.

One by one the buildings in North Hibbing were lifted onto sleds. Some buildings were small and easy to move. Others were big and difficult to move. It took more than a month to move the Colonia Hotel. Some buildings never made it. The Sellers Hotel slipped off its sled and collapsed.

Everything had to get out of the way of the mines.

Frank Dear's home was lifted onto a platform for the move south.

Others, like the county court-house, were never moved. They were destroyed and rebuilt farther south.

It took ten men to move a building as big as the Dears' house. Two men operated the steam tractor, one at the controls and a second—sitting up over the front wheels—to steer. Other crew members had to help with the sled and make sure the house was secure.

The Sellers Hotel fell from its platform and collapsed during the move.

Imagine moving buildings with a tractor for a mile or more, along unpaved roads. What dangers and problems would the movers face?

You're in Charge of the Move

Just imagine that you are the boss of that moving crew. Your job is to see the Dears' house moved safely from one place to another. You will have to plan a route for the move and give directions to your crew.

First, find the original location of Frank Dear's home on the southeast corner of Center Street and 2nd Avenue near the north end of old Hibbing. Then, locate its destination on the northeast corner of Cody Street and 3rd Avenue. The new address will be 2126 3rd Avenue.

Now, use the maps and photographs of Hibbing to write instructions for your crew. Tell them how to prepare the house for moving. Give directions for the move. What streets will they use? How far will they travel in each direction?

What buildings and landmarks will they pass? How fast do you think they should go? What problems can they expect? What advice can you give to your crew?

When you finish your report, read it in class or compare it to others. Are your directions accurate? Have you used all the information in the maps and photographs? Would your instructions get the Dears' home safely to its new location? Make any changes necessary to complete the job.

Everyone who lived in Hibbing during those years saw the town move, piece by piece, to make

room for the mines. The moving continued until 1958. After that, the valuable ore seemed to run out. The town and the land around it continued to change. New buildings and roads were built. People still moved in and out. But the Village of Hibbing stayed in the same place.

The new town of Hibbing was built south of its original site. Many of the buildings were set on new foundations. The Dear family home was one of them. New construction seemed to be everywhere. Use the map to describe the move of Frank Dear's home from Center Street at the north edge of town, to the corner of East Cody and 3rd Avenue, south of the railroad tracks.

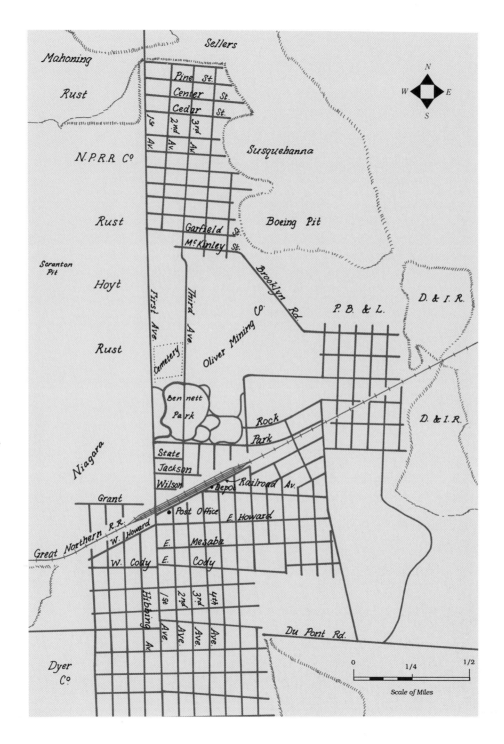

Activity 4
Putting History in Order

There's an old saying that one thing leads to another. That's not quite true. It would be more accurate to say that one thing leads to many others. That's what makes history so interesting. Learning how events affect each other is like reading a good story.

Good stories and good history have something in common. Both depend on the order of events and the relationships between events and people. In stories, that's called a plot. In history, it's a *sequence of events*.

Arranging things in sequence—from the first to the most recent—helps you understand how and why events occurred. For example, each book by Laura Ingalls Wilder is fun to read. But when you read the books in sequence they become more interesting.

The pictures and stories arranged in order help you to understand the changes in Laura's family. You learn why they moved and about the changes in small towns as more settlers moved west.

Putting events in sequence is usually easy. Think of four or five events in your life. Then arrange them in order—from the first to the last. That's all there is to it.

Keeping events in order becomes more difficult as your subject gets bigger. One way to organize events in sequence is to make a *timeline*. A timeline is like a ruler divided into years instead of inches. Each measurement on a timeline represents a date. Events arranged by date on your timeline will be in sequence.

You can learn to use a timeline by working on the history of a small town. Currie, Minnesota, is a good place to start.

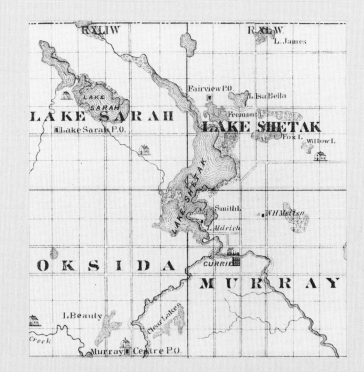

Currie is in southwestern Minnesota, in Murray County, about ten miles northeast of Slayton. About 350 people live in Currie, and another 300 live on farms nearby. Minnesota Highway 30 is on the south edge of town. The Des Moines River is on the north. East and west of town are beautiful farmland and prairie. The map was drawn in 1873.

This photo of the Currie family, relatives, and friends was taken at a summer resort on Lake Shetek near Currie, Minnesota, in 1897. Photographs are firsthand information of events that have occurred in the past. They are called primary sources. What can you learn about the family from this photo?

Reference Books Can Help

Begin with information from *reference books*. Reference books have facts and figures like the size and location of a place, or the date of an event. Encyclopedias, dictionaries, and atlases are reference books.

Here is some information about Currie found in reference books at the Minnesota Historical Society. You can add it to your timeline.

From *Minnesota Geographic Names* by Warren Upham, first published in 1920:

Currie, the village of Murray Township, was founded in 1872, when Neil Currie and his father, Archibald Currie, built a flour mill here, using waterpower of the Des Moines River. This village, which was the first county seat, from 1872 to 1889, being succeeded by Slayton, was named in honor of Archibald and Neil Currie. Neil Currie built the first store here in 1872, and aided in organizing the Murray County Bank in 1874.

Town residents in front of Neil Currie's store, about 1898. What clues to the town's history can you find here?

Minnesota's population was counted every five years from 1850 to 1910. Some towns, like Currie, were so small that the people living there were counted with everyone else in the whole township. Murray Township included the village of Currie and the farms around it.

From the *Census of the State of Minnesota:*

Year	Population of Murray Township
1875	205
1880	288
1885	541
1890	544
1895	575
1900	706
1905	508
1910	488
1915	No census
1920	532

At left is Archibald Currie. Below is the town of Currie about 1875.

Information from Secondary Sources

Most people learn about history from secondhand information. They read books or hear stories written and told by others who have studied about the past. Those books and stories are called *secondary sources.* Several books have been written about Murray County and the town of Currie. Here is a selection from one secondary source. Use your timeline to keep these events in sequence.

From "A Brief History of Our Sister Village Currie" by V. Portman in the *Murray County Herald,* 1915:

In August 1880, the most momentous event in our history occurred when Mr. John Sweetman of Ireland came and bought 25,000 acres of land from the railroad company with the intention of settling a large number of families here. Mr. Sweetman sold his land cheap and aided the families for many years. He ad-vertised his land for years and succeeded in gathering here some hundred and thirty families. In 1882 he built a fine Catholic church and priest's house. In the late 1870s, the Presbyterian church was organized and the church built.

During the years 1886 to 1889, there was a bitter argument between Slayton and Currie for the county seat. The records were stolen from Currie. Slayton won the argument in an election by eleven votes on June 11, 1889. After the county

The railroad first built in southwestern Minnesota stopped at Slayton, not Currie. People and their businesses moved to Slayton. The Currie courthouse at right was no longer used when the county seat finally moved to Slayton, too.

seat was taken away, Currie began to shrink. The town was practically at a standstill until 1900.

In 1900, the railroad finished a branch from Bingham Lake to Currie and the town was given a boost. Since that time, Currie has been on the uplift.

Most secondary sources include some information other authors have overlooked. For example, some members of the Murray County Historical Society wrote *A History of Murray County* in 1982. Their book included two events not mentioned in earlier histories. According to them, "Neil Currie built a telegraph line to Tracy, Minnesota, in 1880," and "the first telephones in Currie were installed about 1900." Both events should be added to your timeline.

A railroad line was built to Currie from Bingham Lake in 1900. There is evidence in this 1907 photo of how the train affected business in town.

Primary Sources Are Firsthand Information

Sometimes you need information that isn't found in reference books or secondary sources. Then you have to study *primary sources*. The word *primary* means first or earliest. Primary sources give firsthand information about an event. Photographs, diaries, letters, some objects, and many newspaper stories are primary sources.

The following story is a primary source because it is told by some-one who saw the events occur. From the *Murray County Pioneer*, Monday, June 10, 1880:

On Thursday evening, about 7 o'clock, Murray county was visited by a cyclone that made sad havoc in some neighborhoods. The home of Mr. and Mrs. Michelson was car-ried a number of yards from its foundation with the occupants. Mrs. Michelson was seriously in-jured. The house was entirely de-molished and some parts found several miles away. The school was lifted from its foundation and car-ried about eighty rods. It was totally destroyed. Several hail storms passed through during the storm. Some people reported hailstones that weighed four ounces and were too large to fit in a teacup.

Notices have been posted for a meeting to be held in Currie Hall on Tuesday evening, June 18, for the purpose of voting bonds to build a new schoolhouse in this district.

Was this photograph of the Currie school taken before or after the cyclone described by Mabel Currie? How can you tell?

Information from a primary source doesn't always need a date to put it in sequence. There may be a clue to its date. For example, a newspaper story may mention an event that happened "last year," "a month ago," or "earlier that day." A photograph may give you a clue about the age of a person or thing.

Mabel Currie grew up in the town founded by her father and grandfather. She knew almost everyone who came and went.

When she was nearly 80 years old, Mabel wrote about her memories of Currie. She told good stories about the town's history, but she included very few dates. As you read her story, try to put the events she mentions on your timeline.

From "It Was This Way" by Mabel Currie, 1953:

My grandfather, Archibald Currie, and father, Neil Currie, came to this prairie county looking for a site on which to build a dam and a mill and a store. They came to New Ulm, as far as the railroad was built. Then they went by wagon 50 miles to this place on the rolling prairie. The following year, my mother, my sister Nettie, myself, and my brother Arch came by train to Tracy. We stepped off the train onto the prairie grass. No station had been built. Father was waiting with a team and wagon and we set out for Currie 14 miles to the south.

Members of the Silvernale family in Currie. Can you figure out when this photograph was taken?

41

Father and others soon built a school across the river and millpond. Our school had only one room. There were knotholes in the floor. When all was quiet, a gopher would stick his head up and watch us.

One afternoon walking home we discussed a test we had to take the next day. How we dreaded it. "I wish the old schoolhouse would burn down. I wish a cyclone would blow it away." Sure enough, as mother was getting us ready for bed that night, we looked from our window to see a fearsome sight. Wind was howling around the house. Hail was falling. Over the millpond hung huge funnels of black clouds. They darted to earth again and again. Mother decided we should hurry to the cellar. The next morning no schoolhouse was to be found. Our slates and books were scattered over the prairie. Father's watch, which the young teacher had borrowed, was found soaked with water and stopped at five minutes of eight.

The new schoolhouse was built in town. It had two rooms downstairs and two unfinished rooms upstairs. Now we usually had a man and a woman teacher.

Father and grandfather helped build the Presbyterian church. Our ministers were usually students from the seminary who came for the summer. We concluded that they must be left-overs. The boys said that they timed the prayers of one of them to be 35 minutes long.

Neil Currie took this photograph while his family was on a picnic at Lake Shetek, north of town. Compare it to the one on page 43. Does it provide any information for your timeline?

42

Finding Relationships between Events

The town of Currie grew up around a store and mill built along a river on the prairie. The town's population rose and fell, and people's lives changed with events. Take a close look at the sequence of events in Currie's history. Pick one of those events and list others that seem related to it. Be prepared to tell others in your class how and why those events are related.

A timeline can help you to understand the history of your own town or neighborhood, too. You can collect information about local history from reference books, secondary sources, and primary sources.

Arrange the information you find in sequence on a timeline. Make your timeline fun to look at. Give it some personality. Use pictures. Find old newspaper headlines and magazine covers. Take photographs of people who tell you about their memories. Try to find maps made at different times to show how places have changed.

Arranging events in sequence on a timeline can help you discover relationships between them. You may see a connection between new highways, new shopping malls, and new houses. You might see connections between international events and local events. Putting things in sequence shows how "one thing leads to many others."

A Currie family photograph taken in 1909. Pictured left to right, back row to front, are Dr. Arch Nelson Currie, Helen Hunter Currie, Ned Currie Jr., Mabel Augusta Currie Davies, Nettie Joan Currie Head, Neil Currie Sr., Mary Augusta Banfield Currie, and Margaret Evelyn Currie Goodwin.

Activity 5
Time and Winter Count

Swift Dog was a Dakota boy. He lived on the prairies west of Big Stone Lake more than a hundred years ago. His father, Chief Running Fearlessly, belonged to Sitting Bull's band, the Band of the Bad Bow.

The Bad Bow were part of the Dakota nation. They lived with other bands of Dakota on land between the St. Croix River to the east and the Rocky Mountains to the west. They governed themselves, hunted for food, protected themselves from the weather and their enemies, and raised their families.

As a young man, Swift Dog learned about the history and traditions of his people. He learned to keep track of time and events and the changing seasons of the year, according to Dakota calendars.

Almost everyone keeps track of time. It helps to arrange the things we do. There's a time for lunch, time to be at work or school, and time to go to bed at night. Time is a way to measure things, too. Some games like basketball and hockey are measured in minutes. We measure a trip in hours or days. We measure age in years.

Chief of the Teton Dakota, Sitting Bull, about 1880

Think of a calendar without pages for each month or numbers for each day. Think of a history book without chapters written about years gone by. If you do that, you might be thinking about this calendar of history kept by the Dakota Band of the Bad Bow. The history of each year was remembered with a drawing describing events from winter to winter.

45

Keeping Track of Time

Time is so important that we give every moment a name or a number. Hours, days, months, and years are the names we use. Those names and numbers—we call them dates and hours—help to arrange events in our memory.

Nature keeps its own time. The moon, stars, planets, animals, fish, and plants all move and change in patterns that the Dakota understood. Time was a part of the world around them. The Dakota indicated the time of an event by its relation to natural patterns like the change of seasons.

No one knows just when people began to keep track of time. At first, people drew on stone to record events. Later they used objects like sundials. Now we use electronic equipment.

The calendar we use now is the Gregorian calendar. It was designed in 1582. Like most calendars, it is based on the rotation of the earth on its axis and the time

Nodinens, an Ojibway woman, lived on the Mille Lacs Reservation. She was 74 years old when she described the use of a counting stick:

When I was young, everything was very systematic. We worked day and night and made the best use of the material we had. My father kept count of the days on a stick. He had a stick long enough to last a year. He always began a new stick in the fall. He cut a big notch for the first day of a new moon and a small notch for each of the other days.

Toward the last of winter my father would say: "One month after another month has gone by. Spring is near and we must get back to our other work." So the women wrapped the dried meat tightly in tanned deerskins, and the men packed their furs on sleds or toboggans.

it takes the earth to make one trip around the sun.

Not everyone uses the same calendar. The Russian Orthodox church, Orthodox Jews, and Muslims each use their own calendars for religious celebrations and traditions. The Ojibway kept track of time with a counting stick. One person in the family notched the stick at the end of each day. It helped them plan their work and prepare for each season.

The Dakota had another way of keeping time. Instead of counting

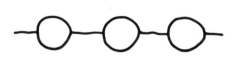

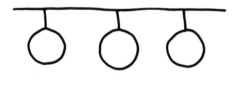

days, they kept track of *nights* or *sleeps*. They often told the distance from one place to another by the number of sleeps it took to travel between them.

They kept track of each month by the changing shape of the moon. They gave names describing seasonal events to each *moon,* or month. The seasons were divided differently for the Dakota, too. Five moons were counted to the winter and five to the summer, leaving one each to the spring and autumn.

The Dakota used circles as symbols of time. A small circle was a year. A large circle was a longer period of time, like a lifetime. Circles connected to a line drawn from right to left showed the passing of time.

The Dakota names for each moon are listed in an 1852 Dakota-English dictionary by Stephen Riggs, a missionary who lived with the Dakota in what is now western Minnesota.

- Wi, a moon or a month
- Psinhnaketu-wi (September), the moon when rice is laid up to dry
- Wi-waźupi (October), the drying rice moon
- Takiyuha-wi (November), the moon of the deer
- Tahećapśun-wi (December), the moon when the deer shed their horns

The Dakota counted the years by winters. Their calendar was a record of events during the past year or winter drawn on the hide of a buffalo or elk. The drawings were called *wa-ni-ye-tu i-ya-wa,* which means *winter count.* The winter count was both a history of the tribe and a calendar. Its drawings represented the most important or unusual event of the past 12 months. The Dakota could tell how old they were by counting from the winters in which they were born.

- Wi-tehi (January), the hard moon
- Wićata-wi (February), the raccoon moon
- Iśtawićayazan-wi (March), the sore-eye moon
- Magaokada-wi (April), the moon in which the geese lay eggs
- Woźupi-wi (May), the planting moon
- Wažuśtećaśa-wi (June), the moon when the strawberries are red
- Ćanpasapa-wi and Waśunpa-wi (July), the moon when the chokecherries are ripe and when the geese shed their feathers
- Wasuton-wi (August), the harvest moon

Swift Dog's Calendar of Time and History

One person in each tribe was keeper of the winter count. The keeper added a picture each year. As he did, he composed and memorized a short story or phrase to explain the new picture. The winter count was passed from generation to generation. Each new keeper memorized the stories that went with every picture.

As a young man, Swift Dog was chosen by the Band of the Bad Bow to keep the winter count. He learned the stories of each year and copied the faded pictures onto a new piece of white cotton cloth. He drew his pictures in black ink and colored them with paint. Each year he added a picture and a new story for the Bad Bow.

In 1913, Swift Dog met a woman named Frances Densmore. She was studying Dakota history and she asked him questions about the winter count. He told her the story of each picture and sang songs about some of them.

Swift Dog told Densmore that he was born in the winter when many Dakota had measles. The phrase that describes that winter is *Na-wi-ćas-li*. Find it on the winter count.

He also told Densmore about the events of *Kan-gí-wi-ća-śta wik-ćem-na-yam-ni wi-ćak-te-pi*. That was the year Swift Dog fought in many battles and killed a man. The winter count phrase means "the year thirty Crow Indians were killed by Dakota."

Swift Dog

Frances Densmore, shown about 1912, collected more than 600 songs of the Teton Dakota. She used a phonograph to record the songs and transcribe the words and music.

Find the winter count picture of that battle. How can you find out how old Swift Dog was when that battle was fought?

It's hard to match the events of Swift Dog's winter count to the dates of our Gregorian calendar. Swift Dog did not include months and years in his drawings. But years before Swift Dog was born, a remarkable event occurred. A Dakota man and a white man both saw it and recorded it on their calendars. This gives us a way to match the events on the winter count to the dates on the Gregorian calendar.

Late in the evening of September 20, 1822, Fort Snelling's commander, Colonel Josiah Snelling, was startled by a brilliant light in the sky. It seemed like an explosion. Later he wrote a letter about the event. "Looking up I saw a meteor. It was uncommonly large and passed so near me that I heard its sound, which resembled that of a rocket. The buildings blocked my view, but I heard it strike the ground. It sounded like an exploding shell, only louder."

Snelling asked a guard whether he had seen anything: "The guard looked frightened. He replied that a large ball of fire had passed very near him, and struck the garden along the river. Other guards saw the same thing."

Farther west, the Band of the Bad Bow saw a shooting star blaze across the sky. They were startled, too, by the brilliant meteor. They talked about it for months. When it was time to add an event to the winter count, the keeper

Na-wi-ćas-li, the winter when many Dakota had measles

No. 171. "Horses I Seek"

Sung by Swift Dog

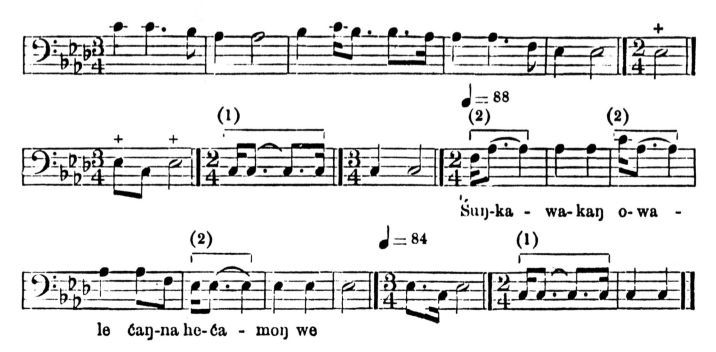

Šuŋ-ka - wa-kaŋ o-wa -

le ćaŋ-na he-ća - moŋ we

Swift Dog wrote this song after stealing horses from a group of Ojibway. He told Frances Densmore that he took a white horse with a saddle on it. He said he had a bow and arrows and shot as fast as he could, but he did not know whether he hit anyone. The words mean: "I do this when I need horses."

49

drew a picture of the star. He called it *Wi-ćan-hpi wan-ho-ton hi-ya-ye,* the winter of the large meteor.

If the meteors seen at Fort Snelling and by the Dakota were the same, the winter of the large meteor is 1822. Then you can match other winter count events to calendar dates. Try it.

Count ahead to the picture showing Dakota people sick with the measles. That is the year in which Swift Dog was born.

Use the same method to find the year in which Swift Dog fought against the Crow and killed a man. How old was Swift Dog when he met Frances Densmore? In what year did the Dakota begin work on this winter count?

Kan-ǵi-wi-ca-sta wik-ćem-na-yam-ni wi-ćak-te-pi, when 30 Crow Indians were killed by Dakota

Wi-ćan-hpi wan-ho-ton hi-ya-ye, the winter of the large meteor

A Winter Count of Your Own

You can keep a winter count, too. Record the events of each school year or the history of your family. Your drawings and stories can pass on the information from one class to the next or from one generation to another.

Begin by organizing your calendar—every year from winter to winter, just like the Dakota. Then think of the events that were part of each year. Which was the most important? Was it something that occurred in your family, at school, or somewhere else in the world? Choose one event for each year. Then decide what you will draw to represent the event.

The keeper of every winter count had to memorize the stories that went with the pictures because the Dakota did not have a written language. Begin by writing stories to go with each picture. Then try to memorize them.

The events and ideas represented by pictures and stories on a winter count remain important to the Dakota. They are a source of history and tradition, of pride and humility, among the people of each band. Swift Dog was not a chief, but his memory was as important as any possession among Sitting Bull's Band of the Bad Bow.

People living in Minnesota before the Dakota, left a record of their lives carved in stone. Some historians think these petroglyphs were made more than 3,000 years ago. Others believe they are only 300 years old. What can you tell about the lives of these people by this evidence?

Activity 6
Digging Up the Past

There was a thin crust of ice on the snow along the riverbank. A layer of fog seemed frozen above the spots of open water. The pale morning sunlight offered little warmth.

Two men trudged their way through the forest along the river. Their fingers were almost numb from the cold and their breath seemed to freeze in front of them. Branches slapping their faces were sharp and painful.

The men had been hunting near a swamp where they shot a deer. They tracked the wounded deer through the snow, and when it fell, they gutted the animal and let it bleed. They were careful, in the cold, to avoid getting wet from the blood. Then they dragged the animal on a sled made of two small trees, through the woods toward their camp.

They pulled the deer across a clearing, into their camp, and alongside their cabin. They butchered the animal and brought the meat inside, where they cut it into smaller pieces and wrapped it in birch bark. They boiled some of the bones for soup and put packages of meat in the back room to keep cold until they needed it.

The men were voyageurs—part of the fur trade—working for a company in Montreal. In 1752 they built a small camp somewhere on the Mississippi, in what is now central Minnesota. There were 10 or 12 men at the camp—or maybe more. The voyageurs and their boss worked for Joseph Marin (Ma-rin), a wealthy and well-known French businessman, explorer, and diplomat. He called the camp Fort Duquesne (Du-kane).

During the winter the voyageurs, Marin, and his clerk lived in their small camp, waiting for the Dakota to bring furs and food for trade. In the summer they traveled—carrying the furs to one of the forts on Lake Michigan, returning with a load of goods for trade. Before the snow fell, they found a new wintering spot and built cabins.

After hunting, the men prepared a meal. They boiled fresh venison and wild rice in a kettle over their fire. They sat at a table and ate directly out of the kettle or off dishes made of wood or bark. The room was smoky.

When the men finished eating, they pushed the scraps aside. Some of the scraps fell to the floor. Small bones were kicked between the floorboards. They threw some of the leftovers into the fireplace and the rest out their front door

onto a trash heap in the snow. The room became cold and dark as the fire burned down.

Their cabin was small, about 16 feet wide and 24 feet long. There were two rooms. The men slept and ate in the larger front room with the fireplace. They used the back room for storage.

The walls were made of logs. Cracks between the logs were sealed with clay and mud. The roof was made of poles, grasses, birch bark, and dirt. The cabin door faced the river.

The voyageurs were the work crew in camp. They built and repaired the buildings and the stockade surrounding them. They did the hunting and gathered firewood. They cleaned the ashes from each fireplace and dumped them with the trash. They wore paths from their cabin, across the yard, past the flagpole, through

Archaeologists excavated this site along the Mississippi River north of Little Falls where evidence of French fur traders was found. Slowly, carefully, they uncovered objects more than 200 years old. Their discoveries provided information about the fur trade, about relationships between whites and Indians, and about the impact of white settlement on the environment.

the stockade gate, and to the river where they collected water.

The boss in camp was the fur trader. He was like the captain of a ship. He gave the orders for trade with the Indians and assigned duties in the camp. He sometimes wore fancier clothes and jewelry, even buckles on his boots. He ate off pottery brought from Europe. He had a clerk to assist him.

The fur trader and his clerk were the upper class of the French fur trade. They had their own cabin. It had glass windows, two fireplaces, and several rooms. The trader and clerk ate and slept separately.

When the Dakota came to trade, the voyageurs helped their boss bargain for furs and food with beads, blankets, jewelry, steel knives, ammunition, and gunflints. They joked and gambled with the Indians and offered them rum and wine to drink.

In the evening, the voyageurs ate again and passed the time telling stories or playing games like checkers and dice. They worked on their guns. Sometimes they gambled. They drank wine or rum. They slept on beds made of straw and animal hides. When the weather was very cold, they got up during the night to keep the fire burning. If they feared danger, they also took turns at guard duty.

Objects like this gun equipment, and pictures like this one of a voyageur, tell something about the way the people lived.

Study this 1830 painting, Indian Women in Tent *by Peter Rindisbacher, to learn how trade with Europeans changed Indian lives.*

Pieces of the Past

The records kept at Fort Duquesne more than 230 years ago have been lost. No diary or pack of letters written there has survived. The buildings have collapsed and crumbled. The best evidence we have of those people and their daily lives is what they lost or left behind.

This story about voyageurs and fur traders came from information recovered by archaeologists. Archaeologists learn about the past from two types of evidence— *artifacts* and *cultural features*. Artifacts are three-dimensional objects, like tools, buttons, or nails. Cultural features are the remains of things built and used by people, like old roads, a house site, a trash pit, or a garden. Archaeologists call both types of evidence *material remains*. They learn to study material remains like the rest of us study books.

Archaeologists often find material remains underground. They carefully uncover them and record every detail of their "dig," mapping the site and showing where each piece of evidence was found. That information is called the *context.*

When they come across some evidence such as a rusty nail or the foundation of an old building, archaeologists ask:
1. What is it?
2. What is its context?
3. How was it made and used?
4. Who used it and when?

The answers to those questions provide information about the way people lived their lives in the past.

Some archaeologists believe this site was used by Joseph Marin's men in 1752 and 1753 for Fort Duquesne. What cultural features did the archaeologists recognize?

Putting the Past Back Together

Now imagine that you were with the archaeologists as they study this campsite along the Mississippi River. Look over their shoulders as they discover each piece of evidence. See whether you can spot information about the French voyageurs and their camp.

Keep in mind the questions archaeologists ask about evidence and its context. Each time you find an object or feature and evidence of how it was made or used, write that down.

The first clue to Fort Duquesne came in a shoebox. A young man from Little Falls brought it to the Minnesota Historical Society. He emptied the contents of the box on the desk of Doug Birk, an archaeologist. Birk took a close look. "Where'd you find this?" he asked.

The young man explained that he found the objects on his uncle's farm, about a mile north of Little Falls, on the west bank of the Mississippi River. He thought the objects belonged to the Dakota or Ojibway who had once lived in the area.

Birk knew the spot. He remembered visiting the site once in 1972. He also recognized the artifacts. They were similar to objects he recovered at other forts built by the French more than 200 years ago. "This is terrific," he said.

These objects and those on page 57, 58, and 59 were found at the site during excavations. Look carefully at each one. Try to answer the questions archaeologists ask about objects they find.

56

Here are some of the objects Doug Birk examined. What can be learned from this evidence? Do you think these objects were left by Indians? If not, who left them behind? Where were they made? Put your ideas in your notebook. Draw a picture or describe the shoebox evidence. What do you think it might prove?

Birk returned to the clearing where the artifacts were found. He brought a crew of researchers from the Institute for Minnesota Archaeology with him. It was hard to see anything at first. The site was overgrown with tall grass and bushes. "We need a lawn mower," said Birk.

After they cut the grass and cleared the brush, the archaeologists could see that the ground was bumpy. They made a map of the site, including the bumps.

They spoke to the land owner and learned that the artifacts had been found in piles of earth and rocks in the clearing near the north edge of the field. "I've never plowed this corner of the farm," he said. "Things you find here have probably been in the same place for a long time."

The IMA archaeologists began to excavate near the rock piles at the north edge of the clearing. Slowly, they peeled away the sod, moved the rocks, and began to sift the dirt. They made maps, drawings, and photographs of the evidence as it was uncovered.

Doug Birk, at left, directed the excavation. Here he photographs cultural remains found on the site. Above, two IMA archaeologists measure and record information about artifacts they have uncovered.

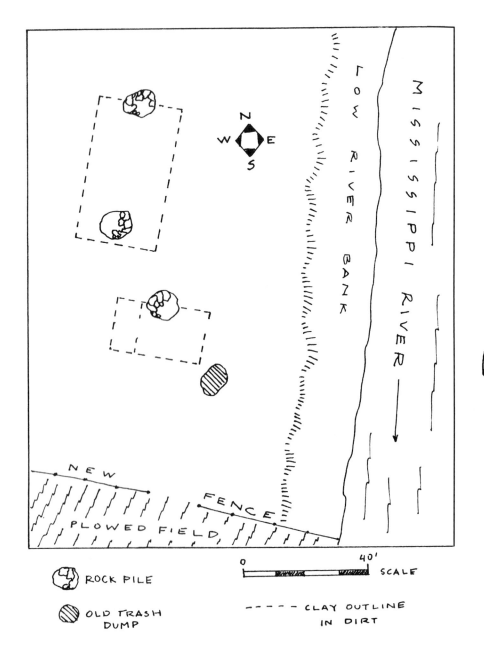

MISSISSIPPI RIVER →

LOW RIVER BANK

NEW FENCE

PLOWED FIELD

0   40'
SCALE

🪨 ROCK PILE

◐ OLD TRASH DUMP

- - - - CLAY OUTLINE IN DIRT

This map was made from the archaeologists' notes and drawings. It shows the position of some cultural remains and artifacts.

They found two rock piles almost 45 feet apart. They studied each feature carefully. Under the rocks were layers of clay and ash. Mixed with the ashes were animal bones.

Then they found something strange. A large rectangular shape seemed to be outlined in the black dirt with clay. The clay lines were several inches deep and about a foot wide. It was about 24 feet wide and 45 feet long. The rocks were piled at opposite ends of the rectangle.

That wasn't all they found. Look at these objects. Do you recognize bits of clothing, personal belongings, or tools?

The IMA archaeologists moved a few feet south. They stripped away the grass surrounding another rock pile. Under the rocks, they found layers of clay, ash, and bones.

They saw another rectangular shape outlined in the ground. They measured it and drew a map. The shape was 16 feet wide and 24 feet long. This space was divided

into two areas. One was larger than the other.

They sifted the dirt, inch by inch. Most of the objects they found were inside the borders of the rectangle. Others were scattered outside, to the east, toward the river.

They found objects made of metal. Some were flat and shaped like tokens. Others looked like small lead marbles. Colored glass beads were everywhere. Sometimes the beads were in clusters, as though they had been spilled.

"Look at this pattern of bones," Birk said. "They're in rows." He was on his hands and knees looking at the ground in the larger area of the rectangle. "I can see four or five rows. The longest row is about six or seven feet long."

Just outside the rectangle, toward the river, they found another feature, It was a small mound made up of artifacts, animal bones, and ash. Things seemed to have been dumped there in a pile.

Objects like those found around the first rectangle were not found here. There were no bits of glass or pottery here. There were no objects made of silver, either.

All of the evidence was added to a map. Look closely at the map and at the artifacts. Imagine how and where the objects were used. Why were some objects found in one place and not in another?

What were those rectangular features outlined in the ground with clay? Why were so many objects found inside the borders of those rectangles? Where did the rock piles come from? Why were they found mixed with the clay, ashes, and bones? How do you explain the animal bones that Birk found lying in rows?

Try to match each piece of evidence to events in the daily lives of voyageurs and traders described in the story.

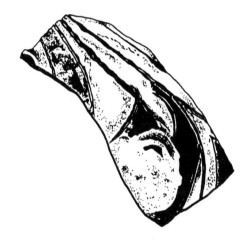

Archaeologists must know exactly where each object is found in relation to others. The exact location of each object is drawn on a map before it is moved.

Is It Really Fort Duquesne?

Archaeologists are careful to collect evidence and record it accurately. They match each new discovery with other information. Their goal is to learn how people lived at times and in places where little or no written record exists.

Doug Birk thinks that the evidence found near Little Falls was left by a group of French traders living in this part of the country over 230 years ago at a place they called Fort Duquesne. "We think this may be Fort Duquesne, but we're still not sure," Birk admitted. "We haven't found an object with Joseph Marin's initials or the year 1752 stamped on it. Nor are we likely to. My guess is based on evidence we found at the site and on a diary written by Joseph Marin in 1753 and 1754."

Joseph Marin wrote in his diary that he sent an employee named Houl to a spot where the Crow Wing River meets the Mississippi, for a meeting with the Dakota. When Houl arrived, he was met by a rival trader, Joseph La Vérendrye (La Vair-ahn-dree). Marin wrote: "La Vérendrye seized all of Houl's trading goods and ordered him to leave. La Vérendrye threatened Houl and warned him not to stop farther south at Fort Duquesne."

That's important evidence for Birk. "It all seems to fit together," he said. "The site is 18 miles south of the spot where Houl met La Vérendrye. All of the objects we found here were made around 1750, probably in France or

IMA archaeologists used a grid to map this part of the excavation. Maps, charts, photographs, and notes are essential because, when objects are removed from the ground, no further information about their original location or their relationship to others may be found.

Canada. We know that this part of Minnesota was claimed by France until 1763. We also know that the Dakota and Ojibway were fighting over this land between 1755 and 1805 and that few fur traders were here during those years. That evidence supports my guess."

What do you think? Have Doug Birk and the IMA archaeologists found the remains of a French fort? Could it be Fort Duquesne? We'd like to hear your opinion. What evidence convinced you that this is the site of Fort Duquesne?

If you are not convinced, what more must be found to prove this site is Fort Duquesne? Write to us. Here's our address:

Northern Lights
Minnesota Historical Society
240 Summit Avenue
St. Paul, Minnesota 55102

We'll write back to you and let you know if more information has been discovered about this site. We'll also tell you about other archaeology going on in Minnesota.

Count the different activities going on at this excavation site. Almost no written evidence of Joseph Marin's business in Minnesota exists. The material remains found here will be used to learn more about French business and politics in Minnesota during the 1700s.

Activity 7
The Adventures of a Fur Trade Canoe

Sunday, July 9, 1820. On the St. Louis River near Lake Superior. We left our campsite this morning and paddled to a place called Knife Portage. Its name comes from the sharp rocks that shoot up from the ground and make it difficult to walk along the shore or paddle canoes through the river.

Although we were as careful as possible, we ran one of our canoes on a rock, hidden just inches under the surface of the black and muddy water.

Fortunately we have an expert guide, Mr. Defour. He is a native of this country, half French and half Indian. Without him, we would find it too dangerous to go on.

There are many rapids here and we depend on the skill of the men in managing the canoes. Sometimes they are in water up to their necks, lifting them over rocks. Next they are in the canoes, setting with their poles to save our whole cargo from destruction.

Charles Trowbridge wrote about that adventure on the St. Louis River in 1820. Trowbridge was an explorer. He traveled through the lakes and rivers that connect Lake Superior with the Mississippi. He and Mr. Defour were interesting people. A story describing more of their adventures would be fun to read.

Another character whose life was filled with interesting events went along with Trowbridge. It wasn't a famous person. It was a canoe!

In those days, canoes were everywhere in northern Minnesota and Canada. Without them there would have been no fur trade and very little exploration. The adventures of a fur trade canoe would make a good story.

It might be impossible to find enough information about an individual canoe to write its life story. Fur trade canoes didn't leave behind much information about themselves. You can, however, cook up your own story about a canoe. Use primary and secondary sources just like the ingredients of a recipe. Add some of your imagination for flavor. For best results, cook the mixture with your knowledge about the fur trade. See what you come up with.

Frances Ann Hopkins painted Shooting the Rapids in 1879. Her paintings are popular for the excitement, beauty, and danger they show. Hopkins sometimes included herself in her paintings. She is the only woman among the passengers in this fur trade canoe.

Getting Started

You need to find ingredients that tell how canoes were built. You need to learn who used them and how. You need to figure out why the canoe was important and how it affected the lives of people. Use words and pictures to tell the life story of a canoe. You might even have the canoe tell its own story.

The primary and secondary sources collected here—the drawings, paintings, artifacts, diaries, maps and other documents—can help you. By the time you finish, you will know a great deal about canoes and why they were so important in Minnesota history.

Some things about canoes are already well known. American Indians built and used canoes long before Europeans arrived in North America. They made some of them by hollowing out the trunks of trees. Others were made of leather or sealskins stretched over a frame of tree branches.

The most common canoes used in the north were made with birch bark. Charles Trowbridge and Mr. Defour used birch-bark canoes. Most European explorers and fur traders depended on the Algonquin and Ojibway Indians to build canoes for them. Later, the Indians taught Europeans to build their own canoes.

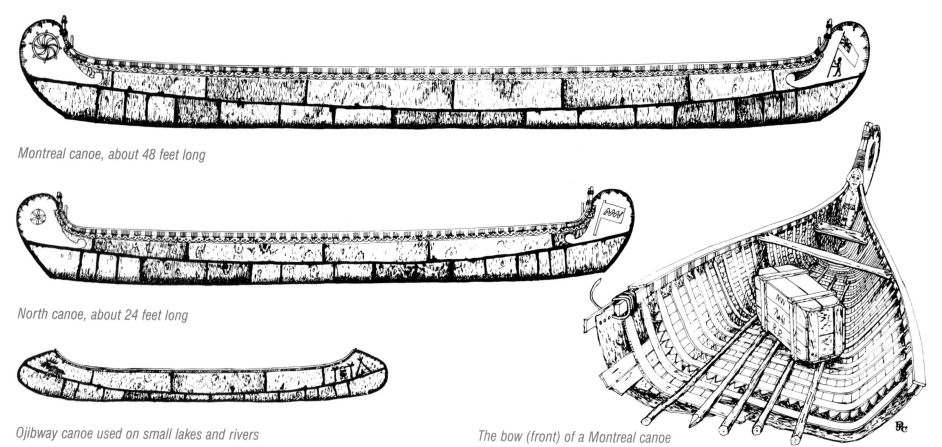

Montreal canoe, about 48 feet long

North canoe, about 24 feet long

Ojibway canoe used on small lakes and rivers

The bow (front) of a Montreal canoe

Fur traders and explorers used three types of canoes in this part of the country. Each was a different size and shape. Some were decorated.

From *The Bark Canoes and Skin Boats of North America* by Edwin Adney and Howard Chapelle, 1964:

Each fur trade route required a special type of canoe. The largest was the Montreal canoe used on the Great Lakes. The smaller North *canoes came into use at the western end of the route. Even smaller canoes were used in the north country where the routes were very difficult to travel.*

Begin your story of a canoe by drawing its portrait. Study the paintings and photographs throughout the activity for some ideas.

Voyageurs paddled a North canoe at Fort William in 1870. Find the fort on the map, on the Canadian shore of Lake Superior.

The voyageurs and their canoes were often in danger. Larger canoes, built for travel on the Great Lakes, were often damaged in the rapids. Frances Ann Hopkins painted this picture, Running a Rapid on the Mattawa River, Canada, in 1870.

65

How Were Canoes Made?

The Ojibway and Algonquin people made canoes according to old traditions. They made their own tools. They used materials found near their homes. This source describes the process. From *The Voyageur's Highway* by Grace Lee Nute, first published in 1941:

The birch bark in the Rainy Lake area is important for the building of canoes. Other trees and plants of great importance to the Indians were the white cedar, the spruce, one of the reeds, and the dogwood.

The wood of the white cedar was used for the framework of their canoes, which were smaller and lighter than the Montreal or the North canoes of the traders. White cedar was also used for canoe paddles.

The roots of the spruce were dug by Indian women, split, and used for thread to sew the seams of canoes. This thread was called wattape, or watab, by the Chip-pewa. The resin of the spruce was used for gumming the seams of the bark canoes.

In 1855, a young writer from Germany traveled to Minnesota and spent time with the Ojibway living near Lake Superior. He watched them build canoes and learned how they were used. Read what he had to say about the way canoes were made. From *Kitchi-Gami* by Johann Georg Kohl, first published in 1860:

An Ojibway woman uses bundles of spruce root as thread to build a canoe.

Boulders keep the bark in place as the canoe begins to take shape.

Wooden stakes are put in the ground to give the canoe shape. Long strips of spruce are used for the canoe's gunwales (GUN-ulls).

I often saw girls, women, and men, all engaged in building and repairing the canoes. Of course, all the sewing and tying—nearly one half the labor—is done only by the women. The men, however, do the paddling, although the women understand it perfectly and are generally more skillful than men.

Use information from these sources to write a description of how your canoe was built. Draw a diagram and label the parts of your canoe. Tell what materials were used for each part and how they were put together.

Ojibway women use spruce or tamarack root to attach the canoe's birch-bark hull to the gunwales.

The bow plate is put in place to add strength.

This Ojibway birch-bark canoe is ready for use.

Where Were Canoes Used?

Fur traders often kept records of their work. In 1777, John Long wrote about his trip from Montreal, Canada, to Lake Superior. He mentions several places that were important in the fur trade. Draw your own map and draw a route your canoe may have traveled.

From *Voyages and Travels* by John Long, published in 1904:

On the fourth of May, 1777, I left Montreal with two large birch canoes, called by the French, maître canots. There were ten Canadians in each as the number of portages require many hands to transport the goods across the landings. This can only be done on the men's shoulders.

Our canoes were made at Three Rivers. They are about eight fathoms long, and one and a half wide. They were covered with the bark of the birch tree and sewed very close with fibrous roots. Canoes this size will carry four tons each.

As early in spring as the ice will permit, they are brought up to Lachine, a village nine miles above Montreal. At this place the trading goods are put on board very carefully.

Canoes were also used for trade. The Ojibway living near Rainy Lake built and sold canoes to European traders. In return, they received kettles, cloth, knives, beads, gunpowder, weapons, and blankets. The price of a canoe changed often. One

The trip from Montreal to the west end of Lake Superior by canoe took three months. Montreal canoes were used for the journey from the towns in the East to Grand Portage. Smaller canoes were used on the border lakes. The North canoe was about 24 feet long and was paddled by four to six men. The Ojibway canoe was paddled by two people. One voyageur could carry it on his shoulders.

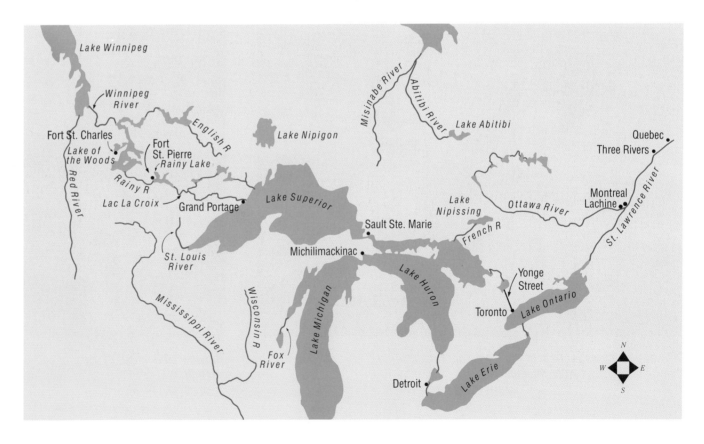

Ojibway man remembered when someone was paid a blanket and 20 yards of cotton cloth for a canoe.

From *Travels and Adventures* by Alexander Henry, edition published in 1901:

On June 10, 1775, I started across Lake Superior from the east with twelve small canoes and four larger ones. Each small canoe was navigated by three men, and each larger one by four.

When we arrived at the Grand Portage, we carried all of our goods across this carrying place. It took seven days of hard and dangerous work.

The canoes used here on the western lakes and rivers are smaller than those which are used between Montreal and Michilimackinac and in Lake Superior. They are only four and a half fathoms in length. It is the duty of the head and stern men to carry the canoe.

Our camp was at the mouth of Rainy Lake where there is a waterfall of forty feet, called Chute de la Chaudière. On the next evening we camped on the Rainy River, where there was a village of fifty lodges of Chippeways from whom I bought new canoes.

Make sure you add Rainy Lake and the Rainy River to your map. Places along the fur trade route are important ingredients for the story of your canoe.

This drawing of a North canoe being unloaded at a trading post was made before 1802.

It took at least two people to carry a North canoe across each portage. Smaller canoes were better for traveling where there were many portages.

A Dangerous Existence

Fur traders and explorers depended on their canoes for their lives and business. But the canoes lived dangerously. They traveled great distances and carried heavy loads. Bad weather and rough country were constant threats. Here is more from *The Journal of Charles C. Trowbridge:*

Monday, May 29, 1820. We paddled with much ease for 30 miles when a violent wind arose. We had to put ashore on a very rocky point, where we succeeded in getting our canoes ashore uninjured. These vessels are so frail that without care the traveler is every hour in danger of losing his canoe, baggage, and perhaps his life. The bark is not more than 1/16 of an inch thick and is stretched over a wooden frame not more than 3/8 inch thick.

Wednesday, June 14. We paddled up the river for twenty miles. We had much difficulty in the numer- ous rapids. In one we injured our canoes so much that it was necessary to land and repair them.

Sunday, July 9. The men were employed last evening repairing the canoes. It is done by applying a composition extracted from the young pine and boiled down to the consistency of pitch, when it is called gum. This is heated and applied to all the seams or openings in the boat, and makes it waterproof.

An Ojibway repairs his canoe at Lake of the Woods in 1912. He uses the traditional materials shown above—spruce gum in a bark container and handmade tools.

What Happened to the Fur Trade Canoe?

Birch-bark canoes didn't have long lives. Some were destroyed in the rapids of a river. Some were dropped and badly damaged on a portage. Others wore out after several years of use. The story you cook up with the ingredients in this activity might include an adventure that threatens the life of your canoe.

By 1890, birch-bark canoes used for trading had almost disappeared. They were replaced by other forms of transportation. The fur trade had changed and no longer needed voyageurs or canoes. These days, fur trade canoes made of birch bark are being saved by the families of those who made them, or are being kept in museums for others to admire.

Voyageurs were fussy about their paddles. Blades wider than five inches were too hard to pull through the water. In length, a voyageur's paddle reached from the ground to his chin. Those in the bow and stern used longer paddles. They also used paddles about eight feet long to run rapids. The paddles were made of birch or maple. The blades and handles sometimes were decorated. The Ojibway women at left, on Leech Lake in 1896, used paddles larger than those of the voyageurs.

Activity 8
Getting to the Land

You can have fun looking at old maps of Minnesota. Sometimes you can find towns that no longer exist or place names that have changed. Some of those maps were drawn from memory by people who traveled and explored in ways we don't see anymore—in boats called bateaux (ba-TOH), mackinaws, and schooners, or with an Indian rig called a travois. Those old maps and the people who drew them led new settlers to this part of the country. They also told people what to expect when they arrived.

In 1805 an American soldier, Zebulon Pike, set out from St. Louis, Missouri. He had orders to travel up the Mississippi River and take notes on what he saw. The government wanted to build a fort along the river, and President Thomas Jefferson sent Pike to find a good spot for it.

Traveling from one place to another was hard. There were covered wagons, stagecoaches, and carts pulled by horses or oxen, but no trains, planes, or boats with motors. Zebulon Pike and his men used keelboats and canoes. Their trip was long, tough, and dangerous. They sailed, paddled, and even pulled their boats up the river. Pike made a map and kept a diary as they traveled:

August 9, 1805. Sailed from our camp near St. Louis at four o'clock with 20 men and enough supplies for four months. The water is very rapid.

Take a close look at Pike's map on pages 74 and 75. It looks different from most maps we use today.

You may find it difficult to use. The title is hard to read. The orientation is unusual. The compass shows north toward the righthand side of the page. No scale is provided on this map, either. That makes it hard to learn how far it is from one place to another.

Pike's map is a primary source. It is firsthand evidence of where his group traveled in 1805 and 1806. That is why this map is so valuable.

Look at Pike's map and find the city of St. Louis, the Missouri River, the River des Moins, and the Ouisconsin, St. Croix, and St. Peter's. (The St. Peter's is called the Minnesota River now.) Find the Falls of St. Anthony, Lake Pepin, Leech Lake, and Lake Winepic (now called Lake Winnibigoshish).

Keelboats were often used on the rivers by travelers arriving in Minnesota Territory.

The travois is a kind of trailer made of two poles tied to the back of an animal. It is loaded with supplies and equipment.

In 1832 Henry Schoolcraft led a group of explorers to the lake they named Itasca. He wrote: "It has a single island where we found old Indian campfires. We saw deer, duck, teal, and loon. Before we left, men cut a few trees and made an area to raise a flagstaff."

Zebulon Pike

This map of the Mississippi River was drawn from Pike's notes and maps made in 1805 and 1806. It begins at the city of St. Louis, where the Missouri flows into the Mississippi. Pike followed the river north to Leech Lake, where he thought he had found the source of the Mississippi.

On September 10 Pike's group camped on an island across from the mouth of what is now the upper Iowa River. There, just about where the southern boundary of Minnesota is today, Pike met with a Dakota chief, Wabasha.

September 10, 1805. When we arrived, the Indians paraded with their guns. They saluted us with three rounds. I had my pistols in my belt and my sword in my hand. I met Chief Wabasha and was in-

vited to his lodge. We talked together and smoked a pipe. He offered me a dinner of wild rice and venison.

Afterwards I went to see a dance that they call their great Medicine. I returned to my boat—sent for the chief and presented him with to-bacco, knives, vermilion and salt.

Pike and his men reached the spot where the Minnesota River (the St. Peter's River on Pike's map) flows into the Mississippi on September 21, 1805. Find it on

Pike's map. There he met the Dakota chief Little Crow and they held a council. Pike wanted to buy land from the Dakota and get their permission to build a fort. He wrote about it in his diary.

September 23, 1805. We began at twelve o'clock noon. I had a shelter built for shade. I gave a speech and three of the Indians replied. They agreed to give me the land—about 100,000 acres—and promised me safe passage. I gave them presents

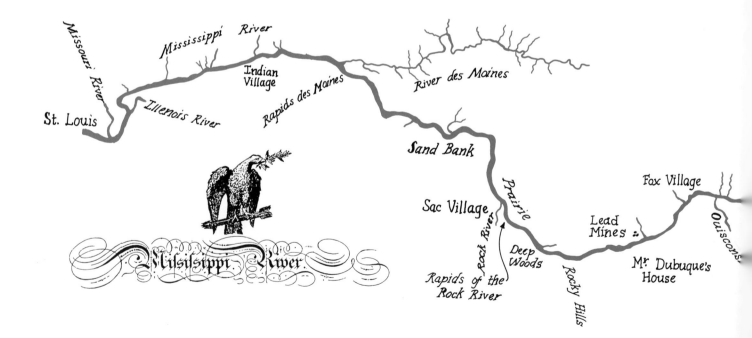

worth about $200. The chiefs said they would sign the agreement, though they thought their word of honor should be enough.

By the end of the council, the Dakota had agreed to give the United States the land for nine miles on each side of the Mississippi, from the mouth of the Minnesota River to the Falls of St. Anthony. They also gave a section of land nine miles square at the mouth of the St. Croix River.

The treaty did not state a price for the land. Pike promised the Indians that the government would pay $5,000 for it later. Little Crow and another chief put their mark on the agreement. Pike signed it, too.

Pike and his men continued north on the river. They wanted to find the source of the Mississippi and to talk with the Ojibway. But on October 3 the temperature dropped below zero. Two weeks later snow fell.

October 16, 1805. It was still snowing and very cold when we woke up. We started out on the river, but after four hours we had made very little progress. We had to wade in the water up to our necks to get the boats through the rapids. Our boats were half full of water. Four men were injured. One had broken a blood vessel. He vomited nearly two quarts of blood. I decided we had to make camp on the west bank of the river south of Pine Creek.

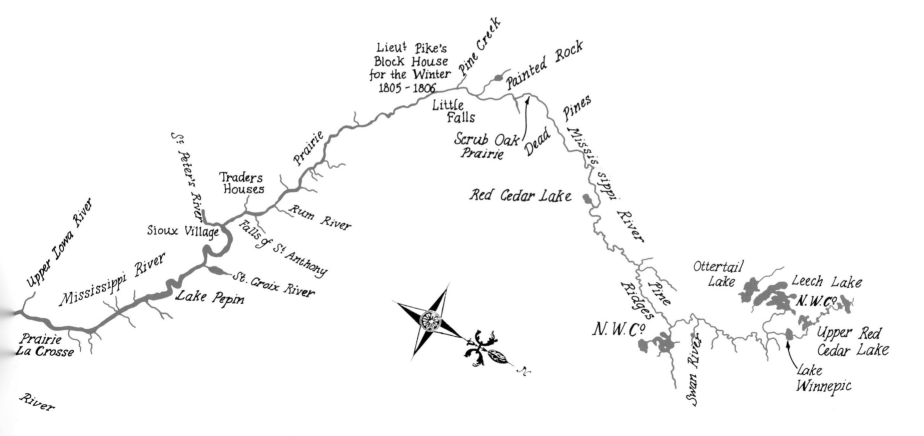

75

Pike and his men were determined. They went on by sled across the snow and ice. Several times they broke through the ice and fell into the river. Once sparks from a campfire started a fire in Pike's tent and burned it to the ground. Often the men were too cold to sleep at night. They hunted for their food. They ate deer, elk, raccoon, buffalo, bear, swan, even boiled moose head and beaver tail.

The men camped along the river at Painted Rock, Red Cedar Lake, and Swan River, and near the present towns of Little Falls, Brainerd, Crosby, Aitkin, and Grand Rapids. They met Indians and fur traders on their way.

On January 31, 1806, the group came to a fork in the river. One branch led north toward Lake Winepic. The men followed the other stream, which turned southwest toward Leech Lake. It seemed to have a stronger current. They thought it would lead to the river's source.

February 1, 1806. We left our camp pretty early. At half past two we arrived at Leech Lake. I will not try to describe my feelings on the accomplishment of my voyage to the main source of the Mississippi.

Pike was excited, but he had made a mistake. The information he had was inaccurate. He followed the wrong branch of the river. He had not found the source of the Mississippi.

Pike and his crew carried their supplies on sleds, in canoes, in boats they called bateaux, and in backpacks. Think of the dangers and problems they faced.

Pike and his men stayed in the north woods through the winter. He talked with the Ojibway chiefs and warriors about making peace with their enemy, the Dakota. He thought he had convinced the two groups to end their fighting.

March 13, 1806. Think of all that could be gained if a great country like the United States used its influence to make Peace instead of spreading the fires of war.

When the ice and snow began to melt, Pike and his group started their trip back to St. Louis. By April 10 they had arrived at the Falls of St. Anthony. Two days later they met Little Crow again at the mouth of the St. Croix River. On April 30, 1806, they arrived in St. Louis, eight months and 22 days after they started.

Other people traveled up the Mississippi River after Pike.

Henry Schoolcraft, Giacomo Beltrami, Lewis Cass, and Joseph Nicollet are the most well known of those who searched for its source. They wrote about what they found and drew their own maps of the area. Their reports encouraged others to explore and settle the territory.

Stephen H. Long

Stephen H. Long was an army officer who explored in the American West between 1816 and 1823. In 1817 he traveled with a crew of seven up the Mississippi to the Falls of St. Anthony. In 1823, he led a group up the Minnesota River, along the Red River, into Canada, and back east through the border lakes and Lake Superior.

On July 23, 1823, Long's group arrived at a fort and trading post of the Columbia Fur Company on the eastern shore of Lake Traverse. Find it on a map of Minnesota. "Soon after our arrival," he wrote, "we were invited to a feast prepared for our party by Waneta—the Charger, who is a chief of the Sioux nation." The next day, the Dakota performed music and danced. Long wrote down the music in his diary, and a member of his group sketched Waneta and his son, at left.

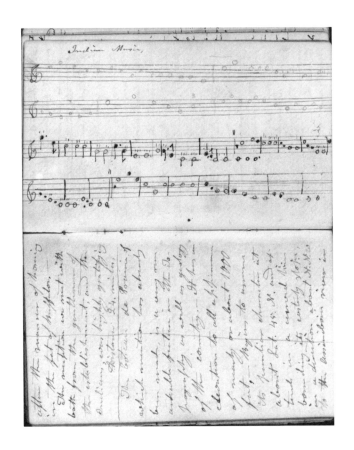

Settlers Come to the Territory

The U.S. Army sent soldiers in 1819 to build a fort on the land Pike bought from the Indians. When the fort was finished, it was named Fort Snelling.

A steamboat made its way up the river to Fort Snelling in 1823. New settlements appeared along the rivers. Afton was settled in 1837, St. Paul in 1838, Cottage Grove in 1844, and Fridley in 1847.

Travel was getting easier. By 1848 you could go by train from Boston to New York City. In 1849 a stagecoach ran from Stillwater to St. Paul and St. Anthony. Some people came to this part of the country by sailing across the Great Lakes in schooners.

In 1850 a young girl named Mary Smith came to Minnesota with her family from Maine. She described how they traveled. Use your own map of the United States to trace their trip to Minnesota.

Use colors or symbols to show the different methods of travel. Add a legend (or key) to show what the different colors and symbols mean.

From Mary Smith Harrison's story in *Old Rail Fence Corners*, first published in 1914:

I came to Minnesota from Lincoln, Maine. I had never been on the railroad or even seen a train. I thought it was the most stupendous machine that was ever going to be in the world. I took my seat and

Mary Smith came to Minnesota from Lincoln, Maine. She traveled on trains, boats, wagons, and carts. Follow her trip on this map. How would a new settler have traveled to Minnesota Territory in 1850 from Pittsburgh, Cleveland, Philadelphia, or Detroit?

bumped along the crazy track. The rails were of wood with iron on top. I have heard my friends say that sometimes the rails came right up through the floor.

At Portland, Maine, we boarded a boat and sailed to Boston. From Boston we took a train again to Albany, New York. Then we boarded a boat for a trip through the Erie Canal. A boat took us from Buffalo, New York, across the Great Lakes to Milwaukee, Wisconsin.

This locomotive was built in the 1850s. It pulled trainloads of people, supplies, and mail to western states and territories.

Travelers like Mary Smith arrived at the harbor in Milwaukee, Wisconsin, on their way west. In 1853, when this picture was made, Milwaukee was not clean and neat. The streets were often littered with garbage and manure.

Mary sailed across the Great Lakes from Buffalo, New York, to Milwaukee, Wisconsin, on a boat like this one.

Milwaukee was a little town. They were just building their sidewalks out of wood. We drove in wagons from Milwaukee to Galena, Illinois. Somewhere in Wisconsin we stopped at a little log hotel. We had heard about rattlesnakes, and we watched out for them in the rooms that night.

We took a steamboat from Galena up the Mississippi. When we got to La Crosse, Wisconsin, some Indians came on board. We landed in St. Paul and took a carriage to St. Anthony.

At St. Anthony we stayed at the Strangers' House. It was a kind of hotel. People who had no place to live were welcome to stay there until they had a place of their own. A French family from the Red River lived in half of the house. We scrubbed out the other half and moved in.

Times have changed since those people came to Minnesota. Dis-

Steamboats stopped at Galena, Illinois, on trips up and down the Mississippi. They were loaded with mail, passengers, cargo, and wood to fuel their steam engines. Mary Smith traveled on the Nominee *from Galena to St. Paul.*

coveries in science and technology have made travel faster and more convenient. Now Mary Smith could take a plane from Maine to Minnesota. Her trip would take only a few hours. Zebulon Pike could use boats with motors to make his trip easier. Accurate maps would keep them from getting lost.

Draw a map of a trip you have taken. Use different colors to show the different ways you traveled (car, airplane, train, bicycle, canoe, boat, or walking). Make sure your map has a title, a compass for orientation, your name as the author, a date, and a scale. Then take a few minutes to write about the trip—just like Mary Smith and Zebulon Pike. Tell where you went, how long it took, and what you saw along the way.

People traveled from one town to another in stagecoaches like this, in horse-drawn wagons, and in carts. Mary Smith rode in a carriage from St. Paul to St. Anthony.

New settlers arrived at the St. Paul levee, the center of business in the town.

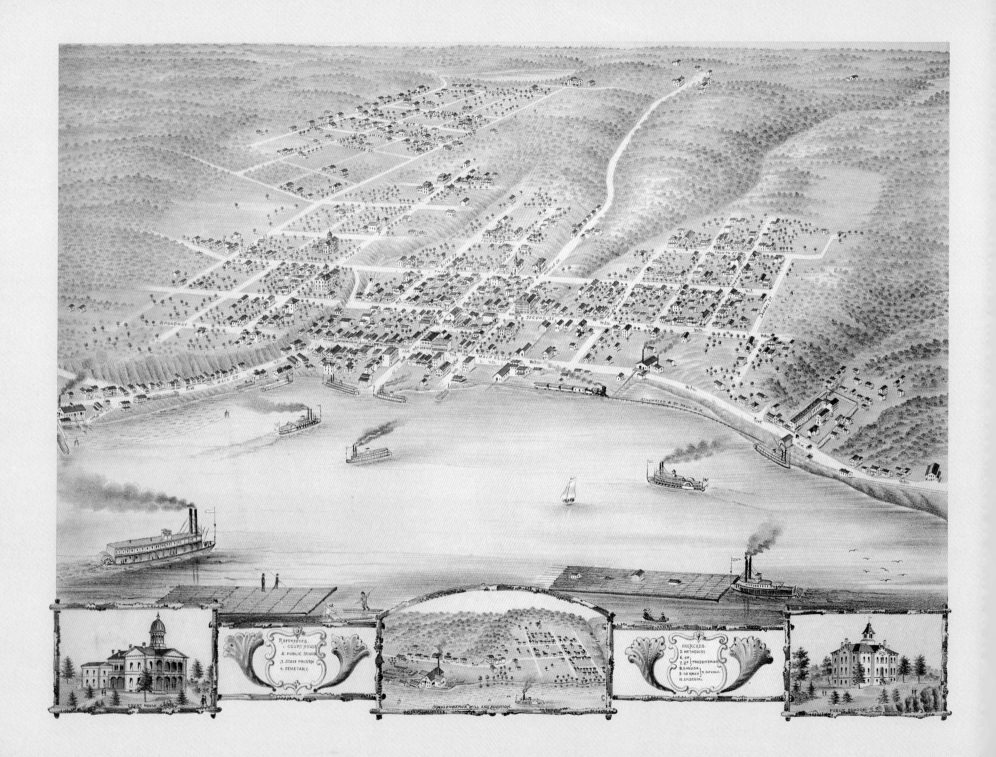

REFERENCES.
1. COURT HOUSE
2. PUBLIC SCHOOL
3. STATE PRISON
4. CEMETARY.

CHURCHES.
5. METHODIST
6. 1ST PRESBYTERIAN
7. 2ND PRESBYTERIAN
8. ENGLISH R. CATHOLIC
9. GERMAN R. CATHOLIC
10. EPISCOPAL.

COURT HOUSE.

SCHULENBERG'S MILL AND ADDITION.

PUBLIC SCHOOL.

Activity 9
Getting Closer to the Truth

Who lived in Minnesota during the 1850s? Where did they come from and why did they settle here? It's not easy to find answers to those questions now. We think there were about 30,000 people living in Minnesota Territory during 1850. Some were Indians whose families had been here for generations. Some were mixed-blood people who were part of the fur trade. Others were white settlers from eastern cities or Europe.

Most of the 6,000 white people lived in small towns or settlements. Some lived on farms. Others lived in places like Fort Snelling or Fort Ripley. Much of the evidence about who they were

and why they came here has been lost. We can still learn about some of the people who lived here. From that information, we can make a good guess about the others.

Stillwater was a growing town in 1850. Its residents settled along a wide stretch of the St. Croix River. White settlers began living and working there about 1843. In 1848, the river became part of the boundary between Minnesota Territory and Wisconsin.

The town grew quickly. When the drawing on page 82 was made in 1870, Stillwater stretched almost two miles from one end of town to the other. Take a close look at the town. What does it tell you about Stillwater and the people who lived there?

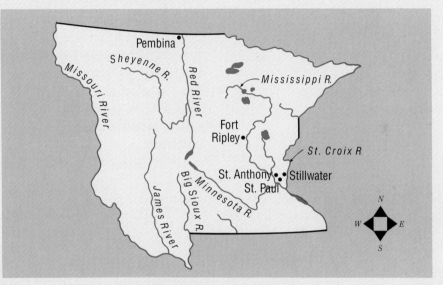

Here's a map of Minnesota Territory as it was from 1849 to 1858. Why were most of the new settlements built along rivers?

Stillwater, already 25 years old, was a busy place in 1870. Find a school, the courthouse, a church, a hotel, the state prison, and at least four different kinds of transportation.

Who lived in Stillwater during the 1850s? Where did they come from? Why did they settle there? Before you look for evidence to answer those questions, make some guesses and write them down. You can make an *informed guess* based on what you learn from studying the 1870 drawing. Historians have a special name for that kind of informed guess. They call it a *hypothesis*. It is a temporary answer to a question or a problem.

You will need more information to see if your guesses—your hypotheses—are correct. Searching for evidence is like solving a mystery. Each bit of information brings you closer to the truth. Every piece helps to solve the problem.

There is plenty of information about Stillwater and its people. Old photographs tell you how it looked. Newspapers tell you what people were talking about. The town's laws tell you what was legal and what was not. Letters,

diaries, and memories that people wrote tell you about their lives.

After you have looked at all those sources, you will know more about the history of Stillwater and Minnesota. You will be able to replace your hypotheses with more accurate information.

Photographs are a good place to look for answers. They show us what Stillwater looked like and what some of its businesses were. The photograph below was taken in 1870.

This scene shows the corner of Main Street and Chestnut. Would you have liked living there? Why might you have decided to stay?

This photograph, taken at the corner of Main Street and Chestnut, shows two hotels. The Minnesota House was built as a private home in 1846. It became a hotel a year or two later. The St. Croix House, down the street, was built in 1848. The photo on page 92 shows the town's biggest hotel, the Sawyer House. It was built in 1868 on the corner of Second Street and Myrtle. John Lowell was the owner.

Stillwater was a busy place. By 1870 people had built homes and businesses along the river on Main Street, Broadway, and Second. There was a courthouse, at least one school, the state prison, and six churches. The information in these photographs may help you learn why people settled in Stillwater.

A town's newspaper is a good source of information, too. Stillwater had four newspapers during the 1850s. They were the *Stillwater Messenger,* the *St. Croix Union,* the *Stillwater Democrat,* and *Rube's Advocate.*

Below is a front page from one of the Stillwater newspapers. When was it printed? Read the headlines. What can you tell about the town from this newspaper? What were the people interested in? What do you think they liked to talk about? How is this newspaper different from those you read? Write down your answers.

The Stillwater Messenger.

VAN VORHES & EASTON,]   "*Be just, and fear not--Let all the ends thou aim'st at, be thy Country's, thy God's, and Truth's.*"   [PUBLISHERS.

VOLUME 2.   STILLWATER, MINNESOTA, TUESDAY, SEPTEMBER 22, 1857.   NUMBER 1.

THE STILLWATER MESSENGER.

A. J. VAN VORHES.]   [W. M. EASTON.

VAN VORHES & EASTON, PUBLISHERS,

Is furnished to subscribers for TWO DOLLARS per year if paid within six months. An additional charge of fifty cents will be made when payment is delayed beyond that time.

Office in Valentine's Building, Chestnut Street.

RATES OF ADVERTISING.

[12 lines, (100 words or less) constitute a square.]

One square, for one insertion,	$1 00
" each additional "	50
One-fourth column, 3 months,	13 00
" 6 "	16 00
" 1 year,	20 00
One-half column, 3 months,	15 00
" 6 "	25 00
" 1 year,	40 00
One column, 3 months,	20 00
" 6 "	35 00
" 1 year,	50 00
Business cards, 8 lines or less, 1 year,	$6 00
" " 6 months,	4 00
" " 3 "	3 00

Advertisements not marked on the copy for a specific number of insertions, will be continued until either by a written or verbal notice, they shall be ordered out, and payment exacted accordingly.

Twelve cents per square will be charged for each change or alteration ordered.

All legal advertisements charged for at rates provided by law.

Displayed advertisements invariably charged extra rates.

DR. E. G. PUGSLEY,

OFFICE, in Curtis' Block, three doors North of the Post Office, Main street, Stillwater.

THE DIFFERENCE.

BY GAIL HAMILTON.

HOW IT WAS TO BE.

I never intended to fall in love
With less than six feet in heighth;
A boundless beard and a fathomless purse
Had always been my delight.

His pale high brow, I said shall be swept
By masses of black, waving hair—
A strange, sad light in the cavernoue eyes,
A shadow, but not of care.

A dark, stern face turned out to the world,
But glowing, turned inward to me;
A heart locked and barred at the stranger's approach,
But I have the golden key.

A voice like the South wind in murmuring love,
Thunder toned in denouncing the wrong,
And a name handed down from the long ago days,
Embalmed in the Troubadour's song.

HOW IT IS.

Well, here we have him. Pray give a glance
To the gentleman *visa-vis,*
Intently engaged with a chicken's wing,
And a cup of his favorite tea.

A round, good natured, full moon of a face,
Eyes blue as the summer's sky;
With the locks on his forehead—well, auburn, at least,
Not to mention a ruddier hue.

He daily toils for his daily bread,
He's the merriest fellow alive;
At eight in the morning, in high-heeled boots,
He measures but five feet five.

He bears in his bosom the biggest heart
On this side of the broad Atlantic;
His chin is as smooth as a lawn in May,
And his name is by no means romantic.

HOW IT CAME TO BE SO.

Exactly! how did it? I really can't tell,

SPEECH OF GOV. RAMSEY.

AT THE

Republican Convention to Nominate State Officers.

Mr. President and Gentlemen of the Convention:—I have been informed by the Committee who have just waited upon me, that I have had this morning, conferred upon me the unsolicited honor of the nomination by this Convention for the office of Governor of this new State of Minnesota. Permit me, Mr. President and gentlemen, to thank you most profoundly. It is well known to all who have conversed with me on this subject, that I would prefer to have served as a common soldier in the army which is to fight the battle of the party and of the country, during this fall campaign. But gentlemen, you have seen fit to think otherwise, and I must say that notwithstanding the personal sacrifices this nomination involves, I am exceedingly grateful for the distinguished compliment.—When I look around me and see this body of highly intelligent men, representing the various interests of this Territory, which has had an existence but for a very few years, I feel that to be selected by you for the office of Governor of the future State of Minnesota, is an honor any man might feel grateful for.

What Slavery has done for the United States.

It has developed a spirit of aristocracy in the nation and brought honest free labor into contempt.

Corrupted our religious organizations, and set up many of our clergy and churches as apologists for a system of oppression, violence, fraud and impurity.

Forced a sectional question into our national politics, and repeatedly endangered the existence of the confederacy.

Plunged the government into a crooked, false and wicked policy, so that it is doubtful whether it ever comes out safe and sound.

Made it honorable to plunder the public treasury and violate the Constitution "for the sake of the Union."

Brought upon us the deserved reproach of inconsistency and hypocrisy abroad, so that the struggling Republicans of Europe no longer trust to the sincerity of our professions, but regard us as the natural allies of despotism.

Made it discreditable to obey the instincts of humanity and the precepts of religion, by opening our mouth for the dumb, feeding the hungry, and doing unto the colored fugitive as we would that men should do unto us.

Involved us in a protracted Indian war.

Andrew Van Vorhes

Here is the front page of the Stillwater Messenger. Andrew Van Vorhes *was its editor.*

85

The Government and Its Laws

The voters of Stillwater elected their first mayor and city council in 1854. The council had a secretary to take notes during meetings and a treasurer to keep track of the town's money.

The members of the city council talked and argued about the laws they needed. Their decisions and laws tell us about the town and the people who lived there. As you read these laws, think about why they were written. Who would have violated the laws? Who was being protected? Who would enforce the laws?

From the town records of Stillwater, 1854:

Hogs Running at Large
If any hog is found running at large within the city limits, the marshal will impound it. The hog's owner must pay $1 within 24 hours. If not, the marshal will post a notice stating that the hog will be sold at public auction in two days. The money will go to the city.

John McKusick was elected mayor of Stillwater in 1854.

What can you learn about a lumber mill and the people who worked there from this photograph of Hersey, Bean, & Brown Lumber Company employees in Stillwater, 1870?

86

Gambling

Anyone convicted of playing at cards, or any other game for money, within the city limits will pay a fine. The fine for a first offense is $5 to $50. The fine for other offenses is $10 to $100.

Prevention of Fires

1. Anyone burning hay, straw, or wood shavings in a city street or lot will be fined $5.

2. Each owner of a building with a stove or fireplace will keep a bucket with the word *FIRE* on it in a public part of the building. If there is a fire, the owner will carry or send the bucket to the place where the fire is. Owners who do not provide a bucket will be fined $1. Any person hiding or destroying a bucket will be fined $5.

Lumber mill owner Isaac Staples

Study this 1870 photograph of the lumber mill owned by Isaac Staples. Find his mill in the picture on page 82. What can you tell about the lumber business from this photograph? How did the mill operate? What can you learn about the people who settled in Minnesota from this evidence?

People and Old Stories

People who came to Minnesota Territory in the early days told good stories about getting here. Stephen Hanks and Jane Black both arrived more than 130 years ago. Stephen Hanks came to work as a lumberjack and riverboat captain. Jane Black and her family traveled up the Mississippi and St. Croix rivers on a small boat from Albany, Illinois. Here are their stories.

From Stephen Hanks's story in *Old Rail Fence Corners*, first published in 1914:

I came in the spring of 1840 from Albany, Illinois, with some cattle buyers and a herd of 80 cattle for the lumberjacks in the woods north of St. Croix Falls. We came up the east bank of the river, following roads already made. In the woods near Chippewa Falls, I found an elk's antlers. I was six feet, and they were just my height. The spread

was the same. They were the finest I ever saw.

When we got to St. Croix Falls, I thought it was a big city. It was quite a town.

In 1843 I helped cut logs, saw them, and raft them down the river to St. Louis. That was the first raft of logs to go down the St. Croix River.

In 1844, we had been up logging in the woods all winter on the Snake River. The logs were all ready for a rain to carry them down

Steamboats began to travel on the St. Croix in the 1830s. The first boats brought people, supplies, and sawmill machinery to logging camps near Stillwater. Boats called Annie, General Pike, Indian Queen, *and* War Eagle *landed at settlements along the St. Croix in the 1840s. By 1851 at least two boats arrived each week in Stillwater. The trip up the Mississippi and St. Croix rivers from Galena, Illinois, took nine days.*

to St. Croix. There was a tremendous amount of them. One day in May, there was a cloudburst. The Snake River overran its banks, and the logs burst away. They swept past everything. They even broke up the sawmill at St. Croix Falls. We built a boom to catch the logs just where Stillwater is today, in still water. Mr. McKusick built a mill there. The lumbermen came, and soon there was a little village. I moved there myself. I was one of the first.

From Jane Black's story in *Old Rail Fence Corners:*

When I came to Stillwater in 1848, I thought I had got to the end of the line. I came up on the steamboat Sentinel *with Captain Steve Hanks. It took ten days to come from Albany, Illinois.*

Stillwater was a tiny, struggling village under the bluffs—just one street. A little later, a few people built on the bluffs. We would climb up the paths, holding onto the hazel-brush to help us up. Stillwater was

headquarters for Minnesota lumbering then.

Sometimes we would get together to have a good time—playing cards or dancing. The mill boarding-house had the biggest floor to dance on. We used to go there often. One of the boys would fiddle awhile. Then someone else would take over and he could get a dance. Sometimes they would dance and fiddle, too.

We often saw bears in the woods. They were very thick. When we took

a stagecoach to St. Paul, it cost $1 each way. Doctor Carli was our doctor. Our bill was only $1 for a whole year.

I have always gone pell-mell all my life. If good luck comes, I take it. If bad luck comes, I take it.

Frederick Schulenburg built this sawmill at Stillwater in 1855.

There's More Information

You've learned a lot of history since you made your first hypothesis about Stillwater. The first guesses you made about the people who settled there may not seem accurate now.

Hypotheses are only temporary answers to questions. They should be changed—or revised—when you learn new information. Think about all the maps, photographs, newspapers, the laws, and old stories you read. Go back to the questions you started with. Who lived in Stillwater during the 1850s? Where did they come from? Why did they settle there?

A census of Stillwater was taken in 1850. It lists 623 residents and gives some information about each of them. Some of the people found in that census are listed below. Study that list and see if it has more information about the people living in Stillwater during the 1850s.

One page from the census will not tell you all there is to know about the people who lived in Stillwater. It does not tell you, for example, whether there were many Indian families in town. It does not provide much information about the work of women. It does give you information about specific individuals and families. The complete census would, of course, provide even more information.

The census is a list of all the people living in an area at a certain time. This was the first one taken after Minnesota became a territory. Seven men were appointed to list the residents. Indians were included only if they lived in white settlements.

Name	Age	Sex	Color	Occupation	Place of Birth
Boutwell, William	47	Male		Missionary	New Hampshire
Boutwell, Hester	34	Female			New Hampshire
Boutwell, William, Jr.	7	Male			Minnesota
Boutwell, Rodney	5	Male			Minnesota
Boutwell, Catherine	3	Female			Minnesota
Boutwell, Hester	1	Female			Minnesota
Boutwell, Basil	9/12	Male			Minnesota
Falstrom, Jacob	44	Male		Farmer	Sweden
Falstrom, Margerite	52	Female	Indian		Lake Superior
Falstrom, Nancy	27	Female	Halfbreed		Lake Superior
Falstrom, Cecilla	15	Female	Halfbreed		Lake Superior
Falstrom, James	13	Male	Halfbreed		Lake Superior
Falstrom, George	6	Male	Halfbreed		Lake Superior
Clover, John	37	Male		Grocer	Tennessee
Clover, Jane	28	Female			Tennessee
Clover, Elizabeth	5	Female			Illinois
Clover, Jacob	1/12	Male			Illinois
Taylor, Margeritte	18	Female			Illinois

If your first hypotheses now seem to be incorrect or incomplete, revise them. Add new information. Take out ideas that seem to be inaccurate.

Hannah Greeley

Elam Greeley

Important information about women is missing from early census lists. The Territorial Census of 1849 includes only the names of men. The 1850 census includes women's names but does not list their occupations. Elam Greeley is identified as a lumberman in the early census lists. Women, like his wife Hannah Greeley, are identified only as "female."

Jonathan McKusick, a relative of Mayor John McKusick, was the census taker for Washington County and all of northeastern Minnesota.

Name	Age	Sex	Color	Occupation	Place of Birth
Ramsden, Thomas	29	Male		House Carpenter	England
Ramsden, Charity	25	Female			England
Ramsden, Thomas, Jr.	6	Male			England
McKusick, John	34	Male		Lumberman	Maine
McKusick, Servia	23	Female			Maine
McKusick, Noah	26	Male		Lumberman	Maine
McKusick, Ivory	23	Male		Lumberman	Maine
Trask, Sylvanus	33	Male		Clerk	New York
Hill, Joshua	27	Male		Lumberman	New Brunswick
Farish, James	30	Male		Lumberman	England
Jackman, Henry	28	Male		Lumberman	Maine
Simpson, Albert	33	Male		Lumberman	Maine
Simpson, Emeline	25	Female			Maine
Kelly, Brigett	19	Female			Massachusetts
Martin, Adam	13	Male		Lumberman	Germany
Ames, Michael	30	Male		Lawyer	Vermont
Ames, Mary	30	Female			Massachusetts
Ames, Eugene	2	Male			Massachusetts

One Last Step

By now you have written, revised, and tested your hypotheses. Your answers about who came to Stillwater and why are based on research and study. The information you collected describes many of the people living in Stillwater during the 1850s. You may conclude that some of those people came to Stillwater looking for work in the lumber business. Many came from New England or other midwestern states. They represented different occupations and backgrounds. Some came alone, and others brought their families.

It is more difficult to learn about all the people living in Minnesota Territory during the 1850s. Who were they? Where had they come from and why did they settle here?

Every town, settlement, camp, and fort was different from every other. Each family and individual

The Sawyer House was the biggest hotel in Stillwater.

had their own reasons for being here. Finding evidence and collecting information about all of those people is probably impossible.

It is possible, however, to hypothesize about people living in Minnesota during the 1850s. The sources you studied and the information you collected about Stillwater can help.

Answer each of the following questions with a hypothesis. Then list two specific sources that would help you learn more about the subject. Tell where you would find those sources. Finally, tell what you could learn from each source.

1. Who lived in Minnesota during the 1850s?
2. Where did they come from?
3. Why did they settle in Minnesota?

Remember, your sources do not have to be the same as those used to study Stillwater. You can use artifacts and other material remains. Some of the sources might be found far from Minnesota. Information about the past comes from many different types of evidence. Use your imagination and experience. These are all important tools when you're looking for truth about the past.

The corner of Main and Chestnut streets in the summer of 1870

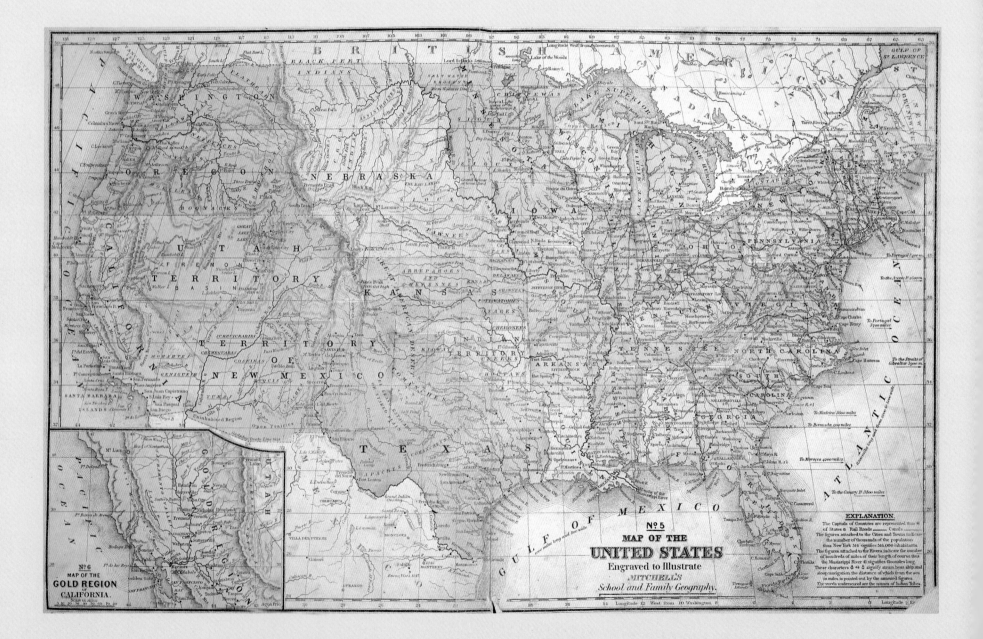

Nº 5
MAP OF THE
UNITED STATES
Engraved to Illustrate
MITCHELL'S
School and Family Geography.

Nº 6
MAP OF THE
GOLD REGION
OF
CALIFORNIA.

EXPLANATION.
The Capitals of Countries are represented thus ●
of States ◉ Rail Roads ____ Canals
The figures attached to the Cities and Towns indicate
the number of thousands of the population
thus New York 516 signifies 516,000 inhabitants.
The figures attached to the Rivers indicate the number
of hundreds of miles of their length of course thus
the Mississippi River 41 signifies 4100 miles long
These characters ⚓ signify steam boat sloop and
sloop navigation, the distance of which from the sea
in miles is pointed out by the annexed figures.
The words underscored are the names of Indian Tribes.

Activity 10
Three Scenes from the Civil War

On Saturday, July 12, 1862, a group of Union soldiers camped near the small town of Murfreesboro in Tennessee. Early the next morning, they were attacked by Confederate cavalry. Soldiers from the Third Minnesota Regiment were among the Union troops who were surrounded and forced to surrender. Madison Bowler—a young man from Nininger, Minnesota—was one of the soldiers taken prisoner.

The battle and surrender at Murfreesboro had a lasting effect on the lives of those soldiers. Military battles, however, are only one way that war can touch our lives. While soldiers from Minnesota were away from home, their families and friends were lonely. They made sacrifices for the war, too.

Members of the government worked hard to end the war. Senator Henry Rice from Minnesota, President Abraham Lincoln, and others struggled every day to solve the complicated problems that caused the war.

Three Scenes from the Civil War is based on information found in documents written during the years 1860 to 1865. It dramatizes events and emotions people experienced during the war. It is different from everything else you will read in *Northern Lights* in two important ways. First, it is written like a play—with a cast of characters and stage directions—that may be read aloud or performed. Second, *Three Scenes from the Civil War* is *historical fiction*.

Historical fiction is usually an imaginary story based on the lives of real people and actual events. The author may include events and conversations or describe a person's thoughts and emotions without evidence to prove they happened. Unlike history, historical fiction may include events that did not actually occur.

The characters in this play are real. The Battle of Murfreesboro really happened. The play is considered to be fiction, however, because some of the events and conversations have been made up. Some of the words spoken by the characters were found written in their letters, speeches, and other documents, but there is no evidence to prove these events happened as they are described here.

CHARACTERS

MR. SAMUEL CALEFF
MRS. SUSAN CALEFF
MRS. STONE
ELIZABETH CALEFF
EUGENE STONE
MADISON BOWLER
NICK O'BRIEN
COLONEL LESTER
ARTILLERY SOLDIER
SECRETARY OF STATE
    WILLIAM SEWARD
SENATOR CHARLES SUMNER
PRESIDENT LINCOLN
WHITE HOUSE SERVANT
SENATOR HENRY RICE

Students used this map of the United States in 1856. Slavery was still legal in some states. Madison Bowler and Elizabeth Caleff agreed slavery should end and the Confederate states should return to the Union. The two are pictured on their wedding day, during the Civil War. The letters they wrote reveal their feelings for each other and about the war.

Scene One: The home of Samuel and Susan Caleff in Nininger, Minnesota. Mr. Caleff is talking with a neighbor, Mrs. Stone, in the living room.

MR. CALEFF *(calling upstairs).* Elizabeth!

MRS. CALEFF *(calling upstairs as she enters the living room from the hall).* Elizabeth! Mrs. Stone is down here with a letter for you.

MR. CALEFF *(to Mrs. Stone).* Come in and sit down.

MRS. STONE. I can't stay. I just wanted to deliver this letter. I know everyone looks for mail from the boys.

MR. CALEFF. What do you hear from your son?

MRS. STONE. I haven't had a letter from Eugene for more than two weeks. They were in Nashville, guarding the capitol. He said that they expected to move east. They heard that people out there are loyal to the Union. *(Elizabeth Caleff enters the room from the hallway, eager for the letter.)*

MRS. CALEFF. Mrs. Stone has a letter for you from Madison.

MRS. STONE *(handing the letter to Elizabeth).* Here's what you've been waiting for. *(Elizabeth*

Madison Bowler sent this picture of himself to his sister from an army camp.

Posters like these encouraged men to enlist in the Union army. Madison volunteered soon after the war began.

(takes the letter and opens it.)

MR. CALEFF. What does he say, Lizzie?

ELIZABETH. They're in Tennessee—at Murfreesboro— near Nashville. He sent a picture of himself and one of a friend, too.

MRS. STONE. When can he come home?

ELIZABETH. It doesn't say. He always writes about coming home, but he says he won't leave until the war is over. It's his sense of duty. He says he enlisted to conquer the enemy and save the Union, and he'll stay until that happens.

MR. CALEFF *(to Mrs. Stone).* You should hear what he has to say about the war. All of the men in his family are Democrats, but Madison sure sounds like a Republican.

MRS. CALEFF. I don't think anybody in his family voted for Lincoln.

MR. CALEFF. But Madison believes in the Union. That's why he joined the army. He says the troops can't wait to fight.

What can you tell about Elizabeth from these letters addressed to Madison in 1861?

Officers of the First Minnesota Regiment at Fort Snelling, May 1861

97

MRS. STONE. My Eugene thinks it will be over soon.

MR. CALEFF. Madison seemed to think so, too, for a while. He says the rebels lost a lot of good men. But he hasn't been so hopeful lately. The government's calling for more volunteers now, and it doesn't look so good.

ELIZABETH (*looking at the letter*). He's heard about our women's group. He says if it weren't for the work of volunteer women, even more boys would die in the hospitals.

MRS. STONE. The paper says Lincoln's plan is to block all the southern ports, send troops down the Mississippi, and attack from the north. How long can the rebels hold out?

ELIZABETH (*reading from the letter*). Listen to this. "Secession has changed everything here. The hand of war can be seen everywhere. Homes are destroyed and deserted, fields

Slow steamboats brought supplies, food, and mail to troops. Their crews were in danger from enemy fire. in November 1863, the crew of the Chattanooga *delivered supplies to Union soldiers at Kelley's Landing on the Tennessee River, just six miles from the town of Chattanooga, Tennessee.*

laid to waste, fences burned. Helpless women and children are left in poverty to get along by themselves. The roads are strewn with decaying carcasses of horses and cattle and hogs killed by rebels during their retreat from the Union army." It sounds dreadful.

MRS. STONE. Have they taken any prisoners?

ELIZABETH. I don't know. Once he wrote about a group of prisoners he saw taken at Summerset. They were a sorry lot—dirty and ragged. He said he pitied them more than hated them. It's terrible. I wish this war were over.

MRS. STONE. These times will change, Lizzie. The President said he will do anything to win the war. By the time Madison comes home, the railroad will be built across the state. Then you two can get married and homestead on good land.

MR. CALEFF. Let's hope it's Union land and that the president is a Republican.

A front-page article in Harper's Weekly *described the work of volunteers in hospitals near the fighting. The article was published June 29, 1861.*

Union troops depended on the work of volunteers to collect, pack, and send supplies. Elizabeth and Madison wrote to each other about the work of organizations like this Soldiers' Aid Society.

Scene Two: Sunday, July 13, 1862, in a Union army camp at Murfreesboro, Tennessee. Madison Bowler is with his friends Nick O'Brien and Eugene Stone.

EUGENE. Get down, Madison. The rebs are coming up from the woods.

NICK *(excited and nervous)*. Over there, on the left. Near the river.

MADISON. How many are there, Nick? Can you see?

(Confederate cavalry gallop into view and toward the Union troops.)

COL. LESTER *(shouting from his position behind the troops)*. Prepare the artillery. Third Regiment, prepare to fire!

EUGENE. Get to some shelter, Madison. Find cover. They're using shotguns!

ARTILLERY SOLDIER. Field artillery ready to fire, sir.

COL. LESTER. Fire at will!

NICK. Let 'em have it!

(The explosion of gunfire and artillery is deafening. Yelling and shouting adds to the confusion.)

ARTILLERY SOLDIER. Fire again!

EUGENE. Nick, you've been hit.

NICK. Stay down, Eugene. I'll be okay.

ARTILLERY SOLDIER. Fire!

(The Confederate troops ride full speed between two groups of Union soldiers and shoot at them with double-barreled shotguns and revolvers. Bullets hiss through the air. When the cavalry charge is over, men and horses lie dead and dying in front of Bowler and his friends.)

EUGENE. They were so close you could touch 'em.

MADISON. Did you hit anyone, Nick?

This photograph was given to the Minnesota Historical Society by Edna Bowler in 1963. A note on the back reads: "Five members of the 3rd Minnesota Volunteers, Co. F, in camp at Nashville, Tennessee, 1862." Do you recognize one of the soldiers? What do you know about the lives of these men?

NICK. You bet I did. If they try it again, I'll get a couple more.

EUGENE. Where'd they all come from? There must 'a been a thousand.

MADISON. I bet they lost 50 men. Why don't we go after 'em now? Finish 'em off.

ARTILLERY SOLDIER. Col. Griggs asked Lester for permission to attack. All he said was, "We'll see."

MADISON. What more is there to see? We can see we won't win unless we fight!

EUGENE. Look! A white flag. It's the rebels. Are they asking for a truce?

NICK. They're talking to Col. Lester. He's riding with them towards their camp. What are they up to?

MADISON. What happened to the Michigan boys? I haven't heard any fire from them for a while.

EUGENE. Do you think they were captured?

NICK. We shouldn't have split up last night. They had no defense against that cavalry.

MADISON (impatiently). I can't understand this. Why don't we take the fight to them? I'm sick of the way we're fighting this war.

NICK. You've been hit, too, Eugene. Your leg is bleeding.

EUGENE. It doesn't hurt so much. I'll get it wrapped later.

(The men continue to wait while Col. Lester talks with the Confederate officers. It seems like hours before the men see Col. Lester appear again.)

ARTILLERY SOLDIER. Look. He's

back. Over there. Lester's talking with Andrews and the other officers.

EUGENE (very surprised). He's carrying the flag of surrender. I don't believe it. Lester has surrendered. We're prisoners!

MADISON. How can that be? They ran from us.

NICK. They have the Michigan troops, too. Their commander has given up and he's convinced Lester to do the same.

MADISON. God have mercy on the Union. We've been disgraced.

Murfreesboro, Tennessee, in 1862. The Third Minnesota Regiment fought and was captured here by Confederate cavalry.

A soldier of the Confederate cavalry

Scene Three. Several days after the battle at Murfreesboro. President Lincoln is meeting with Secretary of State William Seward and Senator Charles Sumner of Massachusetts at the White House.

SEWARD. The news on every front is discouraging, sir. The Union needs a victory—something to hold off the critics and keep the Union together. This war isn't going to end soon.

SUMNER. We can't wait any longer to do something about slavery. Why can't we take some action? *(There is a knock at the door. A White House servant enters.)*

SERVANT. Excuse me, Mr. President. Senator Henry Rice of Minnesota is here to see you.

LINCOLN. Thank you. *(Pause.)* Come in, Senator. I'm glad you could come over.

RICE. Is it safe for a Democrat in a room full of Republicans?

SUMNER. It's safer here than with our troops in Virginia.

RICE. More bad news?

LINCOLN. There's not much else these days. What have you heard, Rice? What about the Minnesota regiments?

RICE. The First Minnesota was with General McClellan and the others in Virginia. They were one of the few bright spots in that week of terrible fighting outside of Richmond. They won a skirmish or two, but their losses were high.

SEWARD. What about out west?

RICE. The Third Minnesota was in Tennessee—guarding Nashville. There were plans for them to move east, but I just heard they surrendered after a battle at Murfreesboro.

LINCOLN. Do you have any details? What happened?

President Abraham Lincoln with General George McClellan and Union officers near Antietam Creek in Maryland, September 1862

RICE. They were with some troops from Michigan and Pennsylvania. There were about a thousand Union soldiers, but their camp was divided and poorly guarded. They were surprised by Georgia cavalry. There was fighting and the Michigan boys took heavy losses. They were surrounded and forced to surrender.

LINCOLN. Not a very encouraging report.

RICE. With due respect, Mr. President, the field hospitals are filled with wounded and sick boys. Troop morale is low. The Union needs a victory.

LINCOLN. We haven't lost the war yet, Senator. We're fighting to save the Union and we'll do what's necessary to accomplish that.

SUMNER. You know how I feel, Mr. President. There's no longer time for compromise. We can't save the Union without ending slavery.

SEWARD (surprised). What are you suggesting, Sumner? Freeing the slaves before the war is over?

SUMNER. Nothing would help more.

SEWARD. Freeing the slaves could cost you the next election, Mr. President.

LINCOLN. There are others who say if we do *not* free the slaves, it will cost us the *war*. I'm not sure who's right. When I've made up my mind, I'll talk about it with all of you. In the meantime, Senator Rice, what can we do for the Third Minnesota?

RICE. A prisoner exchange. Our boys for theirs.

LINCOLN. We'll try it. Seward, get started on it. If things go well, it should be done in a month. Let me know how I can help. Good night, gentlemen, and pray for the Union.

(Curtain)

Senator Henry Rice of Minnesota

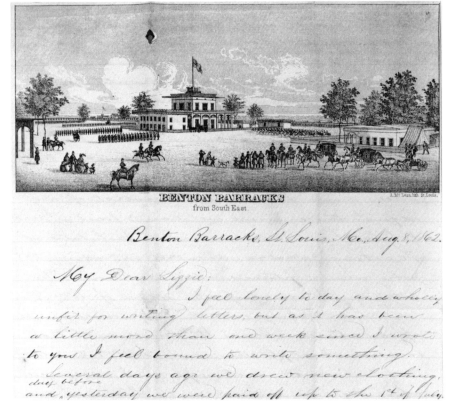

Shortly after he was released by the Confederates, Madison wrote several letters to Elizabeth from Benton Barracks near St. Louis. He told her the men were "downhearted" about their "shameful surrender."

An End to the War

Soldiers from the Third Minnesota Regiment captured at Murfreesboro were released in a prisoner exchange a month after the battle. Shortly after their release, the Third Regiment was sent to Minnesota to join in fighting against the Dakota.

President Lincoln discussed ideas for an end to slavery with his cabinet advisors in July 1862.

On September 22, 1862, he issued the Emancipation Proclamation. It provided that on January 1, 1863, "all persons held as slaves within any state then in rebellion against the United States shall be forever free." It was not until the 13th Amendment was added to the U.S. Constitution in 1865, however, that slavery in the United States ended.

Madison Bowler and Lizzie Caleff were married on November 30, 1862. Madison returned to

The Third Minnesota Regiment shared in some Union victories. This painting, The Third Minnesota Entering Little Rock, *by Stanley Arthurs represents one of them. When Madison Bowler returned to the South, he was stationed in Little Rock, Arkansas.*

the South and remained in the army until 1866. He was promoted several times. Eventually he became a major and was stationed in Little Rock, Arkansas. There he commanded a regiment of black soldiers, most recruited from the Confederate states.

By the summer of 1863, Union armies were more successful in their fight against the Confederates. Northerners became more optimistic about the outcome of the war.

Lincoln was re-elected President in November 1864. Five months later, on April 9, 1865, General Robert E. Lee of the Confederacy surrendered his troops to General Ulysses S. Grant after a battle near Appomattox, Virginia. Although some fighting continued until the end of May, the Civil War had ended.

Bowler was away from home during the election of November 1862. He sent his ballot back to Nininger from his army camp. Bowler's friend Otto Dreker was sent on army business from the camp in Little Rock to Minnesota in December 1863. Bowler gave him money to buy silk and linen in Chicago and asked him to deliver the material to Elizabeth in Nininger. At left is the receipt for the material and thread Elizabeth used to make a dress.

Activity 11
Looking for Reasons in History

The Dakota or Sioux Indians agree to sell to the United States all their lands in the State of Iowa and all their lands in the Territory of Minnesota.

Those are the words of an 1851 treaty written at Traverse des Sioux, a small settlement along the Minnesota River. In the treaty the Dakota agreed to sell 24 million acres of land to the United States for about $3 million. That's about 12½ cents an acre. The Dakota also agreed to move onto a reservation along the Minnesota River.

People have always made treaties. They have used some treaties to end wars or avoid fighting. With others, they have set rules for trade or business.

A treaty is made between two people or between groups. A treaty almost always involves an exchange or trade. Everyone involved in a treaty hopes to gain something, and everyone expects to give up something.

The United States has made treaties for as long as it has existed. The U.S. government made two treaties with the Minnesota Dakota in 1851. The first was signed by the bands from western Minnesota at Traverse des Sioux on July 29. The second was signed by the eastern bands of Dakota at Mendota, across the river from Fort Snelling on August 5.

We know a lot about those treaties. Newspaper stories told when and where they were signed. People wrote diaries and letters describing who was there and what they did. An artist drew pictures of the events. That information is clear and easy to find.

It is not so easy to learn why the Dakota were willing to sell their land to the United States. Learning why something happened is often very difficult. Most events have more than one cause.

Let's begin with some primary sources—letters, photographs, and newspaper stories written by people who were there. Study each source carefully. Look for information about the Dakota, the fur traders, the missionaries, and the government.

In January 1850, missionary Stephen Riggs wrote a letter to Governor Alexander Ramsey. Riggs lived near Lac qui Parle in the western part of Minnesota Territory. He had lived with the Indians for 13 years. He knew what it was like to live on the prairie and to depend on hunting and fur traders for food and supplies. According to his letter, the Dakota were having some trouble. What kind of trouble does Riggs describe?

Lac qui Parle
January 14, 1850
Dear Sir,
   There have been reports that the Dakota from Lake Traverse and Big Stone Lake are suffering. They went out in the fall to hunt the buffalo as usual. They have been disappointed. The snow has fallen two to three feet deep. It caught them on the prairie without food and warm clothes.

   A few families have been able to get back to their homes. But most of them are still far out. If they reach home alive they will be able to survive on corn and fish. But they will suffer next spring and summer.

   It would be good if the government could give them some help. A few hundred dollars worth of gunpowder, lead for gunshot, and some blankets will greatly relieve them.
   Yours very truly,
   Stephen Riggs

A year went by, but the Dakota received no help from the government. Instead the United States wanted to make a treaty with the Dakota. It offered to buy land belonging to the Dakota in Minnesota.

Land belonging to the Dakota was sold to the U.S. government in two treaties during the summer of 1851. Frank B. Mayer painted this scene from sketches he made at the ceremony on July 23 at Traverse des Sioux.

Rumors and Plans

Rumors about a treaty began to appear in the newspapers during the spring of 1851. People were talking about the Indians' land. They wondered whether it would be good for farming and what would happen if the Indians sold it to the government. From a story in the *Minnesota Democrat,* May 27, 1851:

If a treaty be made for land belonging to the Dakota, immigration to Minnesota would immediately surpass anything of the kind ever known in the United States, excepting California.

This Dakota country is the most healthy and beautiful land in the country. It is well supplied with water and timber and will be good for farming.

Why do you think the new settlers and people living in towns were so interested in the Dakota land? Write your ideas in your notebook.

Martin McLeod had lived along the Minnesota River since 1837. He traded guns, ammunition, and other supplies to the Indians for buffalo, beaver, and muskrat skins. Then he sold the skins for a profit. McLeod was a friend and business partner of Henry Sibley.

Almost everyone in Minnesota knew of Henry Sibley. He had come to Mendota near Fort Snelling as a fur trader in 1834. In 1849 he was elected to represent Minnesota in the U.S. Congress in Washington, D.C.

Stephen Riggs was a missionary who lived with the Dakota in western Minnesota. He worked as an interpreter at the meetings.

Here is a letter Martin McLeod wrote to Sibley in 1851. It describes some problems McLeod and other fur traders had. Figure out how the fur traders would benefit from a treaty between the Dakota and the United States. Write your ideas in your notebook.

Lac qui Parle
April 26, 1851
Dear Sir,

Business has been very bad recently. Unless the Indians arrange in the treaty to pay what they owe us, we will have a very big loss.

Last fall I had to sell more supplies to the Indians on credit than usual. I had no way to know that it would turn out to be such a bad year. It has been the worst winter for hunting in many years. The oldest among the Indians say that they have no memory of such another.

There is another reason business has been so bad. Rumors about the treaty seem to have disorganized the usual preparations and plans of the Indians. They have done little but talk about the treaty all winter. They seem not to be interested in hunting to pay back what they owe. They just say, "Never mind. It is true we have nothing with which to pay now. But we will pay when the treaty is made."

I am Dear Sir
Very Truly Yours,
Martin McLeod

Martin McLeod came to Minnesota from Canada. He worked for the American Fur Company, trading with the Dakota in the western part of the territory.

The Government Makes an Offer

Henry Sibley, seated below, and his friend Joe Rolette were fur traders. The Dakota owed cash to Sibley and Rolette for goods bought on credit. Why would Sibley and Rolette be interested in the treaty? Governor Ramsey, at right, was the most influential person at the meetings. He decided what would be offered for the Dakota land and how the fur traders would be paid money owed to them by the Dakota.

The government sent Luke Lea (Lee) to Minnesota in June 1851. Lea was the U.S. commissioner of Indian affairs. He was told to convince the Dakota to sell their land and move to reservations.

Lea asked the western Minnesota bands of Dakota to meet him at Traverse des Sioux. He told the eastern bands he would meet them later at Mendota.

Lea and Governor Ramsey arrived at Traverse des Sioux on June 29. Many other people came, too. Newspaper reporters, government officials, fur traders, interpreters, missionaries, and Dakota arrived daily. The government provided food. There was feasting and celebrating.

The meetings began on July 18. Luke Lea made a speech to the Dakota. Here is what he said:

You all know the reason for our meeting. The country you possess is of little value to you, and your Great Father wishes to purchase it. He thinks it would be to your advantage to sell it. There is more land than you can use. It is better for you to settle in a small area where you can have your horses and farms.

Your Great Father will place farmers among you to teach you how to raise corn and potatoes, so *you do not have to depend on hunting animals. He promises you houses to live in, and that your children will be taught to read and write like those of white people.*

Your Great Father will not only pay you a fair price for your land, but he will open farms, schools, blacksmith shops, and provide doctors. Mills will be built to grind the grain you raise for flour.

If you will sell your land, your Great Father will give you money for moving. He will pay you *$25,000 a year for many years. He will also give you money for farming and schools.*

Luke Lea made many promises to the Dakota. Make a list of them in your notebook. Does the government's offer sound like a good deal for the Dakota?

Imagine that you were a Dakota at Traverse des Sioux. What would you have said to Luke Lea?

Artist Frank Mayer was at Traverse des Sioux during the treaty meetings. He filled a notebook with drawings and wrote a diary describing the people and events. Mayer made each of the drawings in this activity.

The Treaties Are Signed

On July 23, 1851, the western bands agreed to sell their land. After each chief and head man signed the treaty, he was led to another table to sign a second document. This one was called the traders' paper. It was an agreement to pay the fur traders money from the treaty for supplies they had sold to the Dakota on credit. Thirty-three Dakota signed the traders' paper, promising to pay a total of $275,000. This is what the traders' paper said:

We, the chiefs, soldiers, and braves of the Sioux Indians, having just made a treaty with the United States and wishing to settle our debts, agree to pay the traders money we owe them as soon as money is paid to us according to this treaty.

Signed: E-tay-wah-ke-an
E-yan-mo-nee
and 31 others

Then the traders' paper listed the traders and the amounts they would get:

Alexis Bailly and	
H. L. Dousman	$15,000
Franklin Steele	3,250
Henry Sibley	66,459
Joseph R. Brown	6,564
Joseph Provençalle	10,066
Alex. Faribault	13,500
Martin McLeod	19,046
Kenneth McKenzie	5,500
Louis Robert	7,490
and 66 others	

A Dakota girl and two Dakota men, drawn by Frank Mayer at Traverse des Sioux

112

After the ceremony at Traverse des Sioux, Luke Lea and Governor Ramsey rode back to Mendota on a riverboat to meet with the eastern bands. There were more speeches and councils about selling land and moving to reservations. After a week of meetings Governor Ramsey asked the Indians to sign: "You have had the treaty explained to you. Have you arranged among yourselves who is to sign first or should we pick one of you to sign it?" No one moved. Finally Chief Wabasha stood up and gave this speech:

You have asked us to sign this paper and you have told these people standing around that it is for their benefit. But I am of a different opinion.

In the treaty you have mentioned farmers, schools, doctors, and traders. To all of these I am opposed.

You see these chiefs sitting here. They have been to Washington before and made a treaty in which the same things were said. But we did not benefit by them. We want nothing but cash for our lands.

You have named a place for our home, but it is a prairie country. I am a man used to the woods, and I do not like prairies. Perhaps some of those here will name a place we would like better.

There were other speeches that afternoon. But before the council ended, the treaty was signed. Dakota land west of the Mississippi River in Minnesota was sold to the government.

Are Frank Mayer's drawings primary or secondary sources? Do you think they are reliable sources of information? What can be learned from this drawing?

Sioux Evening meal - Traverse des Sioux - July 20. 1851.

Time for Conclusions

Why were the Dakota willing to sell their land? Why did the government want to buy so much land west of the Mississippi River in 1851? Look at your notes. The information you found in primary sources should help to answer these questions.

You may have found many reasons to explain why the Dakota and the U.S. government agreed to sign treaties in 1851. That's the way it is with most events in history. There is seldom just one cause or one reason for an event. Almost every occurrence in the past has had several causes. Each contributed to the way things finally turned out.

Write two or three paragraphs about the treaties of 1851. Explain why the Dakota agreed to sell their land, and why the government offered to buy it. You might start by saying: "There are many reasons to explain why the Dakota and U.S. government agreed to the treaties of 1851."

Sleepy Eye (I-śta Hba) was with the Dakota at Traverse des Sioux. He was chief of the Swan Lake Band. When Governor Ramsey and Luke Lea offered a treaty to buy Dakota land, Sleepy Eye made a speech: "Fathers, your coming to ask for my land makes me sad. And your saying that I am not able to do anything with my country makes me still more sad." Four days later, Sleepy Eye and the other Dakota signed a treaty selling their land to the United States government.

The politicians and fur traders knew that Little Crow would have an influence on the treaties. He was chief of the eastern bands and had traveled to Traverse des Sioux to be with his western relatives when they signed the treaty. During the debate at Mendota a few days later, Little Crow reminded Governor Ramsey that the Dakota had not been paid all that was owed to them from earlier treaties.

After several days of talk, Ramsey asked the Dakota which chief they wanted to sign the treaty first. Medicine Bottle spoke up: "There is one chief the soldiers want to sign. He has been a great war chief and our leader. It is Little Crow. We want him to sign first."

115

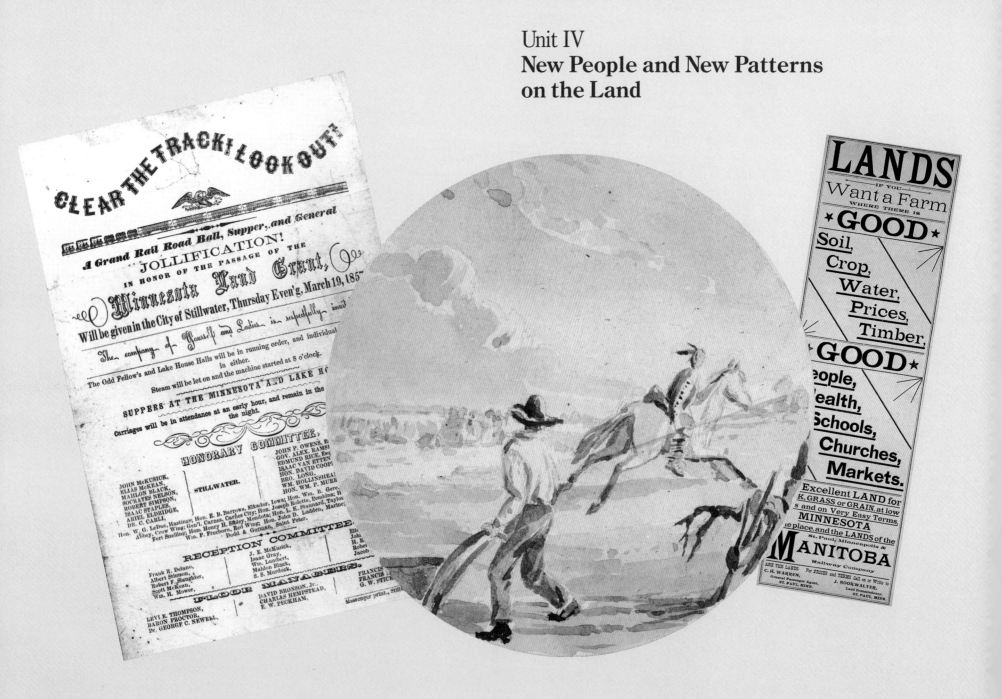

Activity 12
The Business of Settling Down

Lewis and Hannah Stowe came to Minnesota in 1856 for business. They brought some belongings, their three young children, and plans to build and operate a hotel. They settled in Le Sueur County, about 20 miles east of St. Peter. There were other new settlers in the area. Some lived in the small town of Waterville on the south shore of Lake Tetonka. Others lived on farms cleared out of the forest.

Lewis and Hannah didn't waste any time getting started. They claimed 160 acres of land south of the lake. They hired some of their neighbors to help clear land and build the hotel. Lewis kept records of each day's work. He listed the names of everyone who worked for them. Next to the names he wrote how long they worked and how much he owed them. Some men earned 75 cents a day. Others received $1.00. One man, who brought his ox to help pull stumps and logs, received $1.50. Lewis paid some of the men in cash. He promised to pay others with supplies or work.

Work on the hotel started in October 1856. The building began to take shape early in November. The men worked through December. They didn't even take time off for Christmas or New Year's. In January 1857, the hotel was ready for business.

The Stowes began to sell goods and supplies at their hotel. Neighbors bought sugar, coffee and tea, rice, flour, and spices like ginger, salt, and pepper. Some customers paid with cash. Many promised to trade something else for the things they bought. Some agreed to work for the Stowes, clearing land for a garden.

Lewis and Hannah kept records of every expense and receipt. Their records showed a profit in 1857. They could pay their bills.

Running a business and raising a family on the frontier was hard work. Lewis and Hannah kept rooms for their hotel guests. They prepared meals for travelers. They started a garden. They hauled supplies and equipment to Waterville from Winona or Hastings. They had no machines run by electricity or gasoline. There was no train to Waterville. Mail arrived by stagecoach.

Lewis Stowe

Minnesota's new settlers wanted a symbol for the territory. Artist Seth Eastman painted a scene to represent their feelings about settlement in Minnesota. His sketch became the territorial seal and later the state seal. Soon after Minnesota became a state in 1858, railroad companies advertised land for sale and encouraged people to move there.

Lewis and Hannah Stowe sometimes faced difficult decisions. In 1858 the hotel and store were busy. The future of the business looked good. Supplies, food, and equipment, however, were expensive. It was hard to make ends meet without raising crops and some livestock. Lewis and Hannah had to decide whether to concentrate on the hotel or divide their time and energy between the hotel and farming.

Think about the effect each choice would have on their business and family. What would you do?
a. Work hard on the hotel business and try to make more profit.
b. Sell the hotel and move farther west where land is easier to farm.
c. Clear and plant a few acres of land near the hotel. Try to run the hotel, the store, and the farm, too.

If you chose *a*, give yourself three points. Waterville grew quickly between 1857 and 1860. But from 1860 to 1865, during the Civil War and the Dakota War, fewer people traveled through Waterville. The town's population increased very little. The hotel business suffered.

If you chose *b*, give yourself five points. Some settlers did move after living in one place for two or three years. The frontier moved steadily west.

If you chose *c*, give yourself ten points. Lewis and Hannah needed the vegetables and animals they could raise on a farm. Each year Lewis cleared more land. He and Hannah divided their time between working in the hotel, buying and selling supplies, caring for their children, and farming. They grew much of what they ate. Their hotel business provided the cash to buy what they could not grow or make themselves.

Like an advertisement for tourists, the book shown above was written to attract people to Minnesota. When Lewis Stowe arrived in Waterville, he drew the map at right. What are the towns Stowe indicated along the Minnesota River?

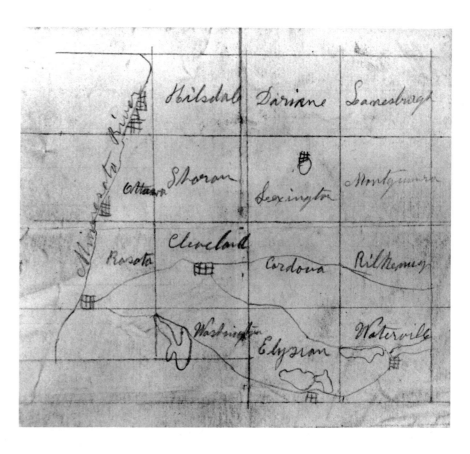

The Stowe farm was similar to others near Waterville. It was small. Most of the land was covered by forest. The trees had to be cut. Stumps had to be burned and grubbed. Rocks and boulders had to be removed before farmers could plow and plant. Most of the farmers in Waterville Township owned more land than they could clear without machinery.

In 1859, the Stowes had a team of oxen, four or five head of cattle, and a few pigs. They couldn't afford to keep horses. Their land, animals, and equipment were worth about $625.00.

In the spring of 1859, Lewis and Hannah were faced with another important decision. They had to choose what crops to plant. They studied all the information about prices and crops. What would you do?

a. Plant only wheat. At harvest use some of the wheat for flour and sell the rest.

b. Plant several vegetables and grains. Use most of the harvest for your family. If some is left over, try to sell it.

c. Plant vegetables only. Use the crop for family and hotel guests. Vegetables can be stored and will last through the winter.

If you chose c, give yourself three points. Wheat was a good crop that could bring a profit. If you chose a, give yourself five points. Frontier farmers needed a variety of crops, however. Their livestock needed grain and corn for feed. Their families depended on vegetables for their diet. That's why the Stowes planted a variety of crops. If you chose b, give yourself ten points.

Sketches by artist Edwin Whitefield, like this scene near Glencoe in the 1850s, are good sources of information. What do you think Lewis and Hannah Stowe's first home in Minnesota looked like?

Lewis Stowe began plowing his fields on April 27. He could plow one acre a day with his team of oxen. (An acre is about the size of a football field.) Next, he harnessed his oxen to a spike-tooth harrow. They dragged the harrow across the ground. The spikes— about five inches long—broke up the clods of earth and made a smooth surface for planting. It took him all day to do just five acres.

He spread seeds for three different types of wheat by hand. Then he dragged the harrow across the field to work the seeds into the dirt. He planted onions, cucumbers, potatoes, two kinds of corn, sorghum, beans, and peas in straight furrows. He finished all his planting on June 14.

Farm families used most of the vegetables, grains, and animals they raised. They ground wheat into flour. They fed oats to cattle and horses, barley to pigs. They

sold what they didn't need. They used the money to buy things they couldn't produce themselves. Sometimes they bought more land. Families able to produce almost all they needed, to buy more land, and to stay out of debt were thought to be very successful.

When the Stowes' wheat crop was ready to harvest, Lewis cut it with a grain cradle. He may have bought the blade in Winona or Hastings. He was a good carpenter and could have made the

PLOWS.—YOU will find at A. LEAMING'S New Shop, any quantity of PLOWS, from a *Great Grub Plow* down to the Corn Plow, and he will also have *Cultivators*, Shovel Plows, Harrows and Harrow Teeth, in order that the Farmers of Minnesota may be supplied with farming implements. All of which he will warrant to give good satisfaction.

☞ *Shop opposite King's Store.*   5–1y

There were no substitutes for a good plow and hard work. Oxen or horses supplied the power.

120

handle. Once the wheat was cut, he had to bind clumps of it by hand. The bundles of wheat were gathered up in bunches of seven, called shocks, and stood up in the field to dry.

When the wheat was dry, Lewis hauled it to the barn. The kernels of wheat had to be separated from the stalk. That job is called threshing. The stalks of wheat were spread on the ground or on the floor of the barn. Some farmers threshed wheat by hitting it with a

hinged hammer called a flail. Others used their horses to walk back and forth on top of the wheat to separate the kernels from the chaff. The kernels of wheat were gathered up and taken to a mill in town for grinding into flour.

After threshing, Lewis had about 100 bushels of wheat. That was more than he needed. He knew he could sell the extra wheat. He read reports in the newspaper that millers in Chicago wanted more wheat from Minnesota.

On his next trip to Hastings, Lewis took some of the extra wheat with him. When he arrived, Hastings was full of people buying and selling wheat. Wagonloads of wheat poured onto the levee. There was wheat in the streets and on the sidewalks. Storehouses were full of wheat. Lewis sold his wheat for about 85 cents a bushel. It was easy to sell. He spent some of the money on equipment for the farm and hotel. Then he bought supplies to sell at his store.

Clearing, plowing, planting, and harvesting with a team of oxen and handmade tools was slow, hard work. New labor-saving equipment was for sale in Winona. Lewis and Hannah knew that a mower pulled by a team of horses could make an easy job of cutting hay. They knew that a reaper could cut and bundle grain faster than anyone doing it by hand.

New equipment and a team of horses were useful on a frontier farm. They were also expensive.

A team of horses and new machinery like this planter made it possible for farmers like Nina Hewitt to work more land and produce surplus wheat to sell for cash.

Lewis and Hannah would have to go into debt to buy them. Many farmers preferred their old equipment and thought it was important to stay out of debt. What would you do? Take a look at the information Lewis and Hannah may have studied, on page 124. What decisions would you make?

a. Buy the new equipment and a team of horses. They will help increase production. If wheat prices stay up, pay off the debt soon.
b. Wait a year to see whether the price of wheat stays high. If it does, buy the new equipment.
c. Try to stay out of debt. Buying new equipment when you don't know what will happen to the price of wheat could get you into trouble. You could lose all your money and your land.

If you chose *c*, you get only two points. The price of wheat was impossible to predict. Making a living without new equipment and a team of horses was difficult. If you chose *b*, give yourself seven points. Many farmers waited awhile to buy new equipment.

The Stowes chose to buy new equipment and a team of horses. They were able to grow more wheat. The price of wheat remained high, and they were soon able to pay off their debt. If you chose *a*, give yourself ten points.

These farmers used horses to thresh the kernels of grain from the stalks of wheat. Before machines with gas or steam engines, farm work was slow and often inefficient.

Other farmers in Waterville Township grew more wheat than they could use at home, too. They knew they could sell their surplus for cash. Some farmers were willing to sell crops in Waterville rather than haul them to a bigger market for a higher price. Others hired someone else to haul their surpluses to Winona or Hastings.

Lewis Stowe made frequent trips to Winona and Hastings with his wagon and team of horses. Other farmers hired him to haul their grain. It was good business for Stowe and a good deal for farmers who couldn't otherwise get their grain to market. Everyone profited.

Agricultural Implement Warehouse.

N. B. & WM. H. STEVENS,

Main Street, cor. Levee,

WINONA,   MINN.

Agents for the Sale of

Kirby Combined Reaper and Mower,

Each new piece of machinery helped farmers work more land. This farmer and his son used a mower to harvest their crops. Farmers depended on high prices for their crops to pay for their equipment.

123

Average Price of Wheat in Winona, 1858–1867

The demand for wheat was growing. Lewis and Hannah thought they could make more money by producing more wheat. They faced another difficult decision. Should they leave the hotel business to become full-time farmers? Study the charts and graphs below to decide.

a. Leave the hotel business. Concentrate on farming and hope the price of wheat continues to go up.

b. Stay in the hotel business. Continue to farm five acres. Use the crops for your family.

Give yourself five points if you chose *b*. Lewis and Hannah could have stayed in business with their hotel and small farm, but their profits may have been small. Give yourself ten points if you chose *a*. Farmers in Le Sueur County were changing the way they did business. They could make more profit by cultivating more land and planting about half of it in wheat. That's what the Stowes chose to do.

Lewis and Hannah Stowe became full-time farmers. They continued to grow vegetables for themselves. They raised some livestock and grew grain and corn for feed. Their biggest crop was wheat. It was their *cash crop*. They grew much more than they could use and then sold the surplus for cash.

By 1868, Lewis and Hannah seemed to have made the right decision. Their farm was busy and profitable. They owned three horses, two oxen, five milk cows,

Value of Farm Equipment and Livestock in Minnesota 1860–1880

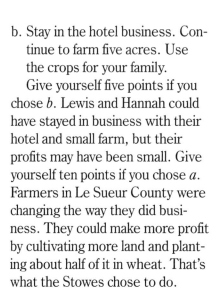

Prices of Some Agricultural Products in Minnesota, 1858–1868

	1858	1861	1864	1868
Corn	.55 bushel	.22	1.25	1.12
Rye	.58 bushel	.33	1.95	1.13
Hogs	4.45 per 100 lbs	3.05	11.75	8.75
Beef Cattle	2.50 per 100 lbs	2.38	4.75	4.00

Prices in dollars

Study this photograph of Winona taken in 1864. What businesses seem to be important in town? Do you think the town grew quickly? How can you tell?

two heifers, seven calves, twelve sheep, five pigs, ten hens, one bull, and a goose. They owned shovels, pitchforks, rakes, hoes, a harrow, a reaper, a mower, a cultivator, and a plow. They had two wagons, a sled, and a sleigh. They had almost $600.00 worth of crops stored in the barn. When they added it all up, their farm was worth $4,255.20.

Lewis and Hannah sold most of the wheat, flour, cheese, butter, lamb, and veal raised and prepared on their farm. Lewis earned more money by working for other farmers. He used his plow, mower, reaper, and team of horses to plant and harvest.

In 1868, the Stowes' total income was $705.69. Expenses for the year were $518.67.

With new machinery and a team of horses, the Stowes could clear and plant more land. By 1870, they farmed 35 acres. They had eight children: David 19, Mary 17, Elizabeth 14, Herbert 12, Alvah 9, Maria 6, Emma 4, and George 7 months. David worked with his parents on the farm. Mary was a teacher in Waterville.

The Stowes added to their house in 1870. They bought lumber, shingles, nails, cement, paint, and wallpaper. They hired men to help with the work. The new rooms were fancier and more comfortable than the rest of the house. When the work was done, they bought an organ for the parlor. It cost $200.00. They paid for everything in cash.

Here's a puzzle: How many years did the Ellefson family live in their home in Hendricks, Minnesota, before this picture was taken? What clues help answer that question?

Francis and I. P. Hill worked at the Minnesota Flouring Mill in St. Anthony. They used these millstones to grind wheat grown in Minnesota into flour.

Lewis and Hannah Stowe became well known in Le Sueur County. In 1872, their neighbors elected Lewis to the Minnesota legislature. He spent most of January and February 1873 at the capitol in St. Paul. When the legislature completed its work, Lewis was offered a new job. He was invited to become the U.S. Indian agent on the White Earth Reservation in northern Minnesota.

Lewis took the job. He and Hannah moved to White Earth. From 1873 until 1878, Lewis helped the Ojibway move onto the reservation. It was his job to see that the Ojibway children attended school and learned to read. He helped the adults to build log houses, farm their land, sell crops, and operate businesses for themselves.

The chance to work at White Earth turned out to be good luck. From 1873 to 1878, many farmers in southern Minnesota fought a losing battle with grasshoppers. Lewis and Hannah missed most of the hardship of those years.

In 1878, the Stowes returned to Waterville. They moved back into their house on land south of Lake Tetonka. They started to farm again. The grasshoppers were gone and the demand for wheat was still growing.

The new railroad through town made a big difference. Farmers could get cash crops to market

This sawmill operated at the White Earth Reservation when Lewis Stowe arrived in 1870. Some of the lumber was used to build houses for the Ojibway, replacing their wigwams.

more easily. Waterville stores sold more supplies and equipment. By 1880, more than 850 people lived in Waterville and more than 16,000 people in Le Sueur County. Sawmills and flour mills were run by steam engines. Almost all farmers plowed their fields with horses instead of oxen. They harvested with reapers and mowers instead of cradles. Most people used cash instead of credit and trade to buy things. Waterville was no longer a frontier settlement. Farmers in

Le Sueur County grew cash crops for markets in cities hundreds of miles away. Times had changed.

Lewis and Hannah Stowe were part of the changes in Minnesota between 1850 and 1880. They made many choices during those years. Their decisions were based on experience and judgment. They were thoughtful and lucky. Business was good and things turned out in their favor.

How did you do? Did your business make a profit during those years? Add up your points. If your score was:

35 points or better, you have a very good mind for business. You study and understand information before making a decision. By 1880, you would have been a successful farmer, business owner, or politician.

29 to 34 points, you were a little slow to make changes from frontier to market farming. Your business probably made a small profit.

22 to 28 points, you survived, but your farm didn't make a profit. You may have taken a job in town or moved west to start again.

21 or fewer points, you had some tough luck. Things didn't go very well in Waterville. You should have moved back East and tried something else. Better luck next time!

Lewis and Hannah Stowe returned to Waterville in 1878. Compare this map with the one Lewis drew, on page 118. What changes have happened since then?

Activity 13
Steam Can Move the World

A century ago, people could only imagine airplanes, spaceships, and rockets to the moon. Back then, travel was limited to horse-drawn wagons, sailing ships, steamboats, trains, and walking. No one knew how to build a machine that could fly through the air at speeds faster than sound.

Long before the first airplane took off, Jules Verne wrote about machines that could fly to the moon and others that could cruise along the bottom of the ocean. His stories mixed imagination with science. They were called *science fiction*.

Jules Verne was a Frenchman. He began writing in the 1850s. His science fiction became popular in the United States and in other countries around the world. He wrote *Journey to the Center of the Earth, Master of the World,* *Around the World in 80 Days,* and many other books.

In one of his science fiction novels, *From the Earth to the Moon,* Verne describes a spaceship shot from a cannon half-a-mile long. The spaceship traveled seven miles every second and arrived at the moon in 97 hours, 13 minutes, and 20 seconds.

In *20,000 Leagues under the Sea,* Verne wrote about an underwater ship, the *Nautilus,* and its mysterious inventor, Captain Nemo. The *Nautilus* was a sleek submarine, faster than any boat ever built. It weighed 1,492 tons. It was 230 feet long and 26 feet wide. It traveled silently underwater around the world.

Captain Nemo bragged about his inventions. His fantastic submarine could even make electricity from the chemicals found in seawater. "I get everything from the ocean. It produces my electricity and that gives the *Nautilus* its heat, light, and movement. In short, its life."

When Jules Verne began writing stories, no one knew how to operate powerful machines with electricity. The newest inventions could produce only enough electricity to make a small light bulb glow dimly. It took time for inventors to catch up with Jules Verne.

Submarines, sea labs, space shuttles, and rockets to the moon are all part of today's world. Scientists spent years learning to design them. They tried hundreds of experiments in building them. Their discoveries and inventions changed *technology*.

Technology is the way people make things. It is the tools, materials, and plans that people use to do their work. Jules Verne made up an imaginary technology for his stories. The tools and machines he wrote about had not been invented yet.

In the 1860s, most work was done by hand or with the help of waterpower, animals, or the wind. A steamboat was the first machine that traveled to Minnesota under its own power. It arrived at Fort Snelling in 1823. No one paddled, pushed, or pulled the boat up the Mississippi. It was powered by a steam engine.

The steam engine was a new technology in 1823. The engine worked by burning wood to heat water. When the water boiled, it turned from a liquid into water vapor—steam. When water turned to steam it expanded, taking up 1,600 times more space. That's when it was put to work. (Just think how much more powerful you would be if you were 1,600 times stronger!)

This painting, The Frozen Mississippi, *was made by Phillip Little in 1910. Imagine walking along the river in front of these buildings 80 years ago. How did steam change the way people lived and worked in the city?*

How Does a Steam Engine Work?

Steam engines aren't complicated. In 1850, they were made of wood and iron. They used water and wood or coal for fuel.

Take out a pencil and some paper. Read this description of a steam engine carefully. Try to draw a steam engine.

The wood or coal burns under a boiler containing water. When the water boils, it turns to steam and expands. The steam forces its way through a small pipe into a tall, round tube called the cylinder. Inside the cylinder is a piston—a steel or iron piece that works like a plunger. The steam forces the piston to move up inside the cylinder. A long rod is connected to the top of the piston. The rod connects above the cylinder to a beam.

The beam works like a teeter-totter. When the piston and connecting rod push up on one end of the beam, the other end of the beam goes down.

The second end of the beam connects to another long rod leading down to a big steel wheel called the flywheel. The rod is attached to a crank near the axle at the center of the flywheel. Each time steam pushes the piston up—forcing one end of the beam up and the other down—the flywheel makes half a turn.

This locomotive, William Crooks, arrived in Minnesota on a steamboat. Its powerful engine could move people and supplies faster than oxcarts, horse-drawn wagons, or boats. Cities, towns, and farms grew along tracks as soon as they were built. Railroads were the freeways of a hundred years ago.

Each push on the flywheel gives it momentum. The flywheel keeps turning and pushes the rod up again. That forces the beam to move and pushes the piston back down to its original position in the cylinder. Then the process starts again.

The engine works a little bit like your bike. When you push on the pedal of your bike, it moves the crank. The crank turns the sprocket. The sprocket moves the chain, and the chain turns the rear wheel.

On a steamboat, the flywheel is attached to the waterwheel by a chain or axle. Every time the flywheel turns, it turns the waterwheel and pushes the boat through the river or across the lake.

AN AERIAL STEAMER, OR

FLYING SHIP.

INVENTED BY

RUFUS PORTER.

Original Editor of the " New-York Mechanic," " Scientific American," and " Scientific Mechanic."

W. GREER, PRINTER, WASHINGTON. D. C. 1850.

Oliver Evans, an inventor who lived in Philadelphia, Pennsylvania, designed and built this steam engine in 1813.

Rufus Porter was an inventor with ideas that could fly. Born while George Washington was president, he lived in New York. Among his inventions are an alarm clock, washing machine, clothes drier, and sewing machine.

Porter published plans for a steam-powered balloon in 1834. The machine was 350 feet long and filled with hydrogen gas. A steam-operated propeller provided the power. Porter built and flew a small model of the machine in 1847.

Porter improved his design and published the book, *Aerial Navigation,* in 1849. It described a balloon that would carry 50 passengers from New York to California in three days at speeds up to 100 miles an hour. Porter worked on the project for 50 years, but he was never able to build a full-sized balloon.

Putting Technology to Work

By 1860, steam engines were replacing waterwheels, windmills, and hand-operated machines in Minnesota. Some steam-engine inventions worked well. Others didn't. For example, sending supplies 100 miles across Minnesota by oxcart often took two weeks. Joseph R. Brown thought he could build a steam-powered wagon to do the job faster.

In 1859 Brown started work on his machine. He hired a machinist in New York to help him. The parts were made in New York and sent to St. Paul. Then the crates and boxes were loaded on a steamboat and delivered to Brown in Henderson, Minnesota.

The steam wagon arrived in Henderson on Saturday, May 19, 1860. The newspaper editor in town wrote: "We do not hesitate to predict its success, providing a good road is made for it. The only serious question seems to be the power of the machinery." As soon as it was assembled, Brown drove the machine down Main Street. It went forward, backward, and made sharp turns. It was a hit with everyone.

On October 6, 1860, Brown drove the new machine out of town, up the steep hill on the west side of town. It didn't take long to reach Three Mile Creek. The

Brown built another steam wagon in 1862. This one had wheels 10 feet in diameter and 18 inches wide. It could travel five miles per hour. Brown's new steam machine started a trip across the prairie from Nebraska City, Nebraska, to Denver, Colorado, on July 22, 1862. The machine pulled three wagons loaded with five tons of freight and two cords of wood for fuel. Twelve miles from Nebraska City, one of the engine cranks broke. Before Brown could improve the design of his steam wagon, railroads were being built across the country.

Joseph R. Brown

132

ground was soft along the creek. When the steam wagon tried to cross the creek, it got stuck. Brown tried to pull it out with horses, but the steam wagon didn't budge. It was too heavy. Brown and his crew walked back to town. They left the wagon stuck in the mud.

Brown tried again to build a steam wagon that could travel across the country. His work was slow and often interrupted. The work was expensive, too, and it was hard to raise money for the project. Brown died in 1870 before he could finish his work. Trains and automobiles soon made steam wagons unnecessary.

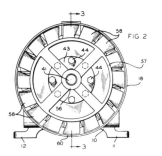

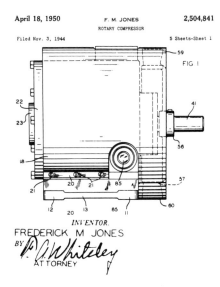

Frederick Jones learned science and engineering from library books and repair shop mechanics. He was a brilliant inventor with little formal education. Jones was just 20 years old in 1912 when he got a job on James J. Hill's farm near Hallock. While he worked for Hill, Jones built race cars, radios, and a sound-movie machine. In 1929, he went to work for a company building recording equipment for sound movies.

In 1935, Jones went into business to organize the Thermo-King Company. He invented special gas-powered automatic refrigeration units for trucks, ships, and railroad cars, like the one at left. Jones made the drawings to patent one of his inventions.

133

Try It Yourself

Now scientists and inventors draw blueprints and write computer programs before they build a new machine. It was different when steam engines were new. Then, inventors just built a model. If it worked, they built more. If it didn't, they tried another model. It was a slow and expensive process. Take a step back in time to learn what that was like.

Think of yourself as a mechanic in 1865. Take a look around you.

Farmers depend on horses and oxen to do the heavy work. Housework is all done by hand. Sawmills and flour mills use waterwheels for power. Steamboats and railroad locomotives are still new inventions.

Think of a way to put your steam engine to work. What farm work can be done with the help of your steam engine? What housework can be done with steam power? How can you cut lumber or grind flour with a steam engine?

Use the steam engine you drew earlier and follow these steps:
1. Decide what job your machine will do. Will it pull something like Joe Brown's steam wagon? Will it push something like a steamboat? Will it turn something fast or lift something heavy?
2. Figure out how to get the power of the piston and the flywheel to do the job. Can you use a chain (like your bike)? Can you use gears (like a car)?

In 1905, threshing on the Sahnow family farm near Bellingham was done with steam power. The kernels of grain are separated from the stalk by a machine operated by the steam engine on a tractor. Compare this crew with the one on page 122.

Identify the parts of this steam engine. Look for the piston, boiler, flywheel, and water source.

3. Draw a model of your invention. Show how it works. Label the parts. Will it stay in one place? Will you have to move it from one place to another?

4. When you finish drawing your steam-engine invention, describe it to someone else in class. Tell how it works. Does it save time? Does it save energy? Does it do a job that can't be done without it? Maybe your partner has an idea that would improve your invention.

Steam engines were an important technology. In the 1800s, they changed the way much of the work was done. Other changes in technology have come along since then. Electricity, gasoline engines, the flight of airplanes, and radio and television are examples. You can probably think of more. Each of those technologies—just like the steam engine—has changed the way people work and live their lives.

Josie Wanous grew up in McLeod County near Glencoe. She worked in a drugstore during high school. After graduation, Josie moved to Minneapolis and went to the Drew Institute of Pharmacy. In 1893 she became the first female registered pharmacist in Minnesota.

Josie had a hard time getting a pharmacy job. She worked as a department store clerk before being promoted to manage the store's pharmacy. She was talented and hardworking. Josie opened her own drugstore on Nicollet Avenue. Her business grew. When Dayton's Dry Goods Company offered her a job, she turned it down. Instead, she expanded her business.

Part of Josie's success came from her inventions. She developed a line of cosmetics and invented a "shampoo bag" using imported and natural ingredients. The shampoo bag and cosmetics were profitable. In 1909 she sold her store, but she produced the shampoo bag until 1936.

Activity 14
History in General

The promise of land and opportunity brought immigrants to Minnesota. They arrived on horseback, in wagons, on trains, and steamboats. Some walked most of the way. They brought clothing and blankets with them. Some packed tools, pots and pans, and kitchen utensils. Some brought along a book, pressing letters and photographs between its pages. They brought high hopes for the future and all the money they had.

Irvin and Orvis Rollins were brothers who traveled to Minnesota Territory from Vermont in 1855. They claimed land in southeastern Minnesota, built a home, and began to farm.

Ole Rölvaag came to the United States from Norway in 1896. He became a teacher at St. Olaf College in Northfield, Minnesota. He wrote novels about Norwegian immigrants. His books captured the excitement of American cities and the loneliness of living on the prairie.

H. P. Lyght and his wife, Stella Jefferson Lyght, brought their three children to Minnesota from Pennsylvania in 1913. They thought homesteading in Minnesota would be better than working in the Pennsylvania mines. They took a train to Duluth and then a steamship along the north shore of Lake Superior.

They stayed with a Swedish immigrant named Alf Nelson at his home near Lutsen for two months. They claimed a homestead of 160 acres in the forest north of there. H. P. built a one-room cabin on their claim. They cleared land, trapped animals, and grew vegetables to support their family.

Though Rollins, Rölvaag, and Lyght came to Minnesota from different parts of the world and at different times, they shared some experiences. Like other immigrants, they were often lonely.

Irvin Rollins kept a diary. He wrote about his feelings in 1855:

It's a little lonesome here—no store, no mail. The cabin leaks a little just to remind me of the stories I have heard of life in the West. There is no church meeting here. It seems odd not to have a Sabbath. I have begun to realize what frontier life must be, but I am not discouraged yet.

Norwegian immigrants and their families held a festival at the state fairgrounds in June 1925. A chorus of singers dressed in red, white, and blue robes formed the Norwegian flag. They sang Norwegian songs to celebrate the hundredth anniversary of Norwegian immigration to Minnesota.

In his novel, *Giants in the Earth*, Rölvaag described the feelings of Beret Hansa, a Norwegian immigrant woman:

Beret had grown more sober as the autumn came, more locked within herself. Her face became more worn and weary. A sense of sadness lay upon her and her appearance seemed to reflect a never-ending struggle. A feeling of deep loneliness settled upon her.

Norman Lyght remembered his family's immigrant experience:

The first several years were very trying, especially for my mother because she was a city-born-and-bred young lady and it was very lonesome for her. She had a hard time adjusting to those living conditions. We were about two miles from the nearest neighbor.

She grew up near Pittsburgh and then moved to the woods. That was a great strain. I can recall her being so lonesome that she would run up and down the trails crying. She was so full of loneliness. It's hard to picture that in history books, but those are the facts. She should be nominated as one of the bravest people in the world.

Irv and Orvis Rollins wrote the shopping list above on the back of a business card. They shopped at Burr Deuel Dry Goods and Groceries in Winona. Twenty years after Ole Rölvaag arrived in the United States, he and his family posed for the photo at right, in 1916.

138

Were All Immigrants Lonely?

Were all immigrants lonely? Probably not. The information in those diaries, stories, and recorded memories represent only three families. It is likely others shared their feelings. It is also likely that some immigrants were not lonely in their new homes.

A statement that summarizes many individual events or relationships is called a *generalization*.

A good generalization tells how things *usually* are. It should be supported by most of the information you can find about the subject. "Immigrants were often lonely" is a generalization based on the evidence left by Rollins, Rölvaag, and Lyght.

Generalizations are an easy way to deal with large amounts of information. They are a kind of shorthand to explain or describe events.

Generalizations don't have to be about history. You can generalize about almost any subject. Give it a try. Make a generalization about your school, your class, about parents, sports, television, or the books you like to read. Just remember the characteristics of a useful generalization:

1. It summarizes many individual events or relationships.
2. It is based on the information you have about the subject.
3. It describes how things usually are.

H. P. and Stella Lyght settled on land near Lutsen and raised their family. They posed for this picture outside their home, probably in the 1940s.

Generalizing about the Past

There are enough sources about immigration history to keep you busy studying for a lifetime. Most people who study immigration history in Minnesota visit the Minnesota Historical Society in St. Paul or the Immigration History Research Center in Minneapolis. They read documents and study objects owned by individual immigrants. They look at photographs and census lists from towns and neighborhoods where immigrants settled. Then they make generalizations about immigrants based on their research.

Here are several sources from two immigrant communities in Minnesota between 1880 and 1920. Some of the maps, photographs, and census lists come from northeastern Otter Tail County. The others are from a neighborhood in St. Paul. Just like Irvin Rollins's diary, Ole Rölvaag's stories, and Norman Lyght's recorded memories, these sources give you an idea of what it was like to be an immigrant in Minnesota.

Study them. Compare them to each other. Then use your new skill to generalize about the past:

- List three different things you can learn about each community from these sources.
- Write two generalizations about each community based on the information in these sources.
- Write two generalizations based on these sources about immigrants in Minnesota between 1880 and 1920.

The sources on this page and the next are from Otter Tail County. The newspaper is written in Finnish. The census information was collected in 1910. The photographs were taken about 1910.

Compare your generalizations with others in class. (Write them on the chalkboard or in your notebook.) Is each supported by *most* of the sources? Does each describe things as they *usually* happened? Does each summarize many individual events or relationships? If your generalizations pass those tests, you have accomplished two goals of a historian. You have learned about immigration history, and you have mastered the skill of generalization. Congratulations!

CENSUS OF PADDOCK TOWNSHIP, OTTER TAIL COUNTY, JUNE 1900

Name	Relation	Age	Place of Birth	Year of Immigration	Occupation	Speak English
Minny, Jacob	Head	45	Finland	1880	Farmer	yes
Elizabeth	Wife	45	Finland	1890	—	no
John E.	Son	17	Michigan	—	Farm Labor	yes
Selma E.	Daughter	15	Michigan	—	—	yes
Fannie	Daughter	5	Minnesota	—	—	—
Lauria, Henry	Boarder	55	Finland	1882	Shoemaker	no
Holt, Mike	Head	33	Finland	1897	Farmer	yes
Severina	Wife	27	Finland	1895	—	yes
John J.	Son	2	Minnesota	—	—	—
Einar W.	Son	1/12	Minnesota	—	—	—
Jacob	Brother	17	Finland	1891	Farmer	yes
Ahola, Charles	Boarder	8	Minnesota	—	At school	yes

A funeral. The man standing may be holding a Bible or prayer book.

The students in this school studied many subjects in Finnish. English was taught as a second language.

141

Italian immigrants settled this small neighborhood along the river, just south of downtown St. Paul, in the 1880s. Most of the people spoke Italian, and the area became known as the Upper Levee or Little Italy.

Photographs can be as useful as written sources in learning about the past. Some people say they can read photographs. They find information in each part of a photograph like others learn from each sentence of a paragraph.

Compare these photographs taken in a St. Paul neighborhood from about 1900 to 1938 with those from Otter Tail County on pages 140 and 141. Read each picture. Look for information in the clothes people wear, the buildings in the background, the people in the picture, the work they do, and the way they pose for the camera.

Family portraits are an old tradition. The Codianni family, which lived in Little Italy, posed for a picture in 1898. Left to right are Giovanni, parents Antonio and Concetta, and Guiseppi. Snapshots are important documents, too. The snapshot of the junior high basketball team at far right was taken in 1936. Most of the boys lived in Little Italy. Their coach, Frank Todora, is in front.

Italian women posed in 1938 with bread from the outdoor oven.

CENSUS OF CITY OF ST. PAUL, WARD 5, JUNE 1900

Name	Relation	Age	Place of Birth	Year of Immigration	Occupation	Speak English
DiJoia, Celestino	Head	75	Italy	1892	—	no
Marie Guiseppe	Wife	68	Italy	1892	—	no
Jannetto, Nicolo	Head	40	Italy	1887	Laborer	yes
Toni	Wife	40	Italy	1887	—	no
John	Son	21	Italy	1887	—	yes
Charley	Son	17	Italy	—	Labor—Tin	yes
Nick	Son	11	Minnesota	—	At school	yes
Frankie	Son	9	Minnesota	—	At school	—
Tina	Daughter	8	Minnesota	1881	—	yes
Yaguina, Langula	Mother-in-Law	64	Italy	—	—	—
LaRisghe, Louigy	Head	22	Italy	1892	Hod Carrier-Plaster	yes
Concert	Wife	27	Italy	1892	—	no
Josephine	Daughter	8	Italy	1892	At school	—
Sammy	Son	3	Minnesota	—	—	—
Rosine	Son	5/12	Minnesota	—	—	—

In Union There Is Strength

Trouble was brewing in the summer of 1893. People were out of work in cities and towns. Farmers were having a difficult time making ends meet. Men and women who had jobs worked long hours for little pay.

Newspapers reported the problems people faced. Headlines told readers "Laboring Men Suffer." Stories described people "glad to work any number of hours at reduced wages."

Business owners were worried. It was hard to make a profit. They looked for ways to save money. Some had to fire employees. Many lowered wages. Most worked longer hours just to break even. They did what they could to stay in business.

Working men and women worried, too. They knew they could lose their jobs or have their wages cut. Often they had no choice but to take what was offered. Some tried to protect their jobs. They joined *unions*—groups of workers willing to take action for higher pay and better working conditions.

Unions had a hard time getting started. Many business owners refused to cooperate with unions. Union organizers were often fired. Their followers were threatened. Violence was sometimes used to frighten union members. Sometimes they had to defend themselves against attack.

Some railroad workers organized small unions called *brotherhoods*. Each brotherhood represented a different kind of railroad worker. The locomotive engineers belonged to one brotherhood. The locomotive firemen belonged to another. The conductors and the mechanics each had their own brotherhood.

Most business owners disliked unions. James J. Hill was one of them. Hill was president of the Great Northern Railway Company, one of the biggest in Minnesota. Hill's company was profitable, and he was a wealthy man. His trains pulled freight, passengers, and mail across the country. The Great Northern Railway stretched from St. Paul all the way across North Dakota, Montana, Idaho, and Washington to the Pacific Coast. Hundreds of men worked for Hill. Some of them belonged to brotherhoods.

Progress toward higher pay and better conditions for railway workers was slow. Some employees became dissatisfied. One of them was Eugene Debs, a locomotive fireman from Indiana.

In the summer of 1893 Debs decided to take some action. He quit his job to organize a new union for railway employees. Debs said

small brotherhoods were not strong enough to bargain with the powerful railway companies. He believed that railway employees needed one big union to bargain as equals with the company owners. He called his new union the American Railway Workers Union.

James J. Hill and Eugene Debs disagreed on how to run a business. Hill thought the owners should make all the important decisions for their company. Debs thought that employees were as important to any business as the owners. He believed employees should be able to bargain with the owners for better pay and working conditions. If the workers joined one big union, he said, they would be strong enough to do it.

As far as James J. Hill was concerned, Debs was a troublemaker. As far as Eugene Debs was concerned, Hill was a villain.

Striking employees of the Great Northern Railway stood in front of a station along the tracks near the Blackfoot Reservation in Montana, April 1894. The station managers gave bread and coffee to the men.

It Depends on Your Point of View

James J. Hill and Eugene Debs had different ideas about what was right and wrong. They disagreed on what was important and what was fair. Each man had his own *point of view*. They understood things differently and acted differently, too.

Everyone has a point of view. The things we think are right and wrong, important, and fair influence the way each of us understands events. Point of view influences the way we act, too.

James J. Hill acted to help his company make money. Eugene Debs and members of the American Railway Union acted to protect their pay and their jobs. The disagreement heated up during the summer of 1893. It boiled over in April 1894, when Debs led the Great Northern workers in a strike against Hill's railway. Hill blamed Debs for the strike. Debs blamed Hill. Which one was right? Was one of them a troublemaker? Was one of them a villain? Your answers depend on your point of view.

On June 20, 1893, Eugene Debs met with 50 railway employees in Chicago, Illinois, to organize the American Railway Union. Unlike the brotherhoods, the new union invited *all* railway workers to form one big union. In the next few months, many Great Northern employees joined the American Railway Union.

At about the same time in St. Paul, James J. Hill decided to cut the cost of operating his railway. He fired some employees and lowered the pay of many others.

In 1893, the Great Northern Railway completed construction of track from St. Paul to the Pacific Coast. At right, James J. Hill adds a spike to celebrate the event.

146

Try to put yourself back in time to 1893 and 1894. Read the speeches and letters of James J. Hill and Eugene Debs. Figure out how to solve their disagreement and settle the strike of April 1894. The first stop on your trip in time is August 1893. That's when James J. Hill writes to all Great Northern station managers:

Gentlemen:

Take whatever steps necessary to reduce service to the lowest point possible. Take off all extra men.

Reduce the wages of others. Keep one or two small gangs of men to pick loose rocks off the tracks. The machinery department, car cleaners, and inspectors should be reduced to the lowest possible level and the same in all station and telegraph service.

- *Reduce all salaries above $5,000.00 per year by 30%.*
- *Reduce all salaries between $2,000.00 to $5,000.00 by 25%.*
- *Reduce all salaries between $1,200.00 to $2,000.00 by 20%.*

- *Reduce salaries of less than $1,200.00 by 15%.*

The rates of wages may appear low, but there will be plenty of men to work at those rates.

James J. Hill

On August 31, 1893, a group of Great Northern workers wrote back to Hill:

We ask that you reconsider your decision to lower our wages. Most of us have families and were already receiving the poorest pay of

Eugene Debs, at left, organized the American Railway Union in 1893 and 1894. Railway employees like those above joined his "one big union."

all railroad workers, only $35.00 to $50.00 per month and working 12 to 13 hours a day, seven days a week. The price of everything including fuel is so high we can hardly exist on our reduced wages.

James J. Hill refuses to change his mind. In January he lowers wages again. In March, he lowers wages a third time. Employees are now paid 30 percent less than in August 1893. Many of the workers complain that they cannot afford the price of room and board—

$26.00 a month—in towns along the Great Northern line. The new pay schedule includes:

Engineers	$80.00 a month
Conductors	$80.00 a month
Brakemen	$47.00 a month
Section Hands	$1.00 per day

On April 13, 1894, members of the American Railway Union protest the Great Northern pay cut. They are willing to strike. Debs's assistant, James Hogan, writes a letter to the general manager of the Great Northern Railway.

Sir:

I am instructed by your employees to say that unless the wages that were in effect before August 1, 1893, are restored, all Great Northern employees will quit work at 12:00 o'clock noon today.

James Hogan

Hill receives the letter only three hours before the strike deadline. He rejects the union's demand. Hill and his managers try to keep things under control. They make plans and send messages to

James J. Hill and his company managers didn't know whom they could trust. During the strike, they sent messages in code. Here is one of the coded telegrams sent to Hill. Someone translated the code, writing in other words above it.

each other in code. Here's one to Hill from a station manager in Montana:

To J. J. Hill:

The smithy tripped night junket, we are occultation running architective tutors except numerously tutors blanch Havre apologees Babylon apologue newly occultation apologue Spokane. The men azure unexpected collitigant limitable George.

The telegram is delivered to Hill's office in St. Paul and translated:

The situation tonight is we are not running any trains except passenger trains between Havre and Butte and between Minot and Spokane. The men left work at twelve o'clock.

On April 14, 1894, Hill sends a letter to the newspaper describing the strike from his point of view:

Some trains on the Great Northern Railway have been abandoned by men quitting work. I received notice only a few hours before the trains stopped running. It is my wish that all employees will go back to work. Those who continue working will be the first to be promoted or receive pay increases. The company is at all times ready to hear and consider any complaint.
James J. Hill

HALT!
—OR THE—
Great Northern Strike.

The pay-cutting serpents have wound their slimy coils around the forms of Labor and his sons.

For this modern Laocoon there is a powerful, keen and trusty blade, and in the hands of St. (A. R. U.) Patrick we trust the snakes will all lose their heads, and not a gash be found on the forms of the sturdy ones who writhe in the awful grip of the only death-dealing serpent we have in these parts.

There was a vast carrying trade and a brilliant vista before the Great Northern when it completed its line from the "Father of Waters" to the Western Ocean; and it celebrated the beginning of its golden era with a horrible gash that was deepest upon those who were the least able to bear it. No tie that labor had not tamped, no spike that labor had not driven; and yet labor, in the hour of strength and triumph, was made the object of a brutal and inexcusable assault.

Did labor bear it patiently? Yes.

And as it sank beneath the blow it got a kick for falling, in the shape of a second reduction in the wage schedule.

Men with fingerless hands and handless arms; men with crushed feet; men with horribly mangled bodies; men who had for years dashed over the ice-covered roofs of flying cars, when blizzards blinded the eyes, and arctic cold clotted the blood in the veins; men who had guided the steed of steel through many a mountain pass where the dynamite of frost and the avalanche of ice have often brought agonized mourning to the humble women and children who depend on the heroes of the rail.

If it is simple justice for the government to pension the men who periled life and limb for it, what is the duty of our railways, and what should the people say to such pay cutting pranks as these enacted by the Great Northern?

We do not know who was responsible for this scheme and its execution, but we do know who can restore to the men that which belongs to them, and that for which they are contending.

Mr. J. J. Hill is a man of vastly more than ordinary ability, and he has a reputation for honor and for liberality that is now imperiled.

By one word from him all will be saved and peace restored.

A hundred wrongs are perpetuated by the customs of railway management, and if this war is carried to the bitter end, every wheel on every railroad may stop until all is righted, and Discretion says, go slow; and all must realize that time should be a great factor in sweeping changes.

This strike has been managed most judiciously, and the men have, with very few exceptions, proved to be law abiding.

We oppose strikes as a rule, but we cannot blame the Great Northern strikers.

If the railroad wins it will pave the way for a more terrible conflict in the future, and there is but one way in which any struggle can find a termination in permanent peace and that is when right prevails.

But the situation at this moment is decidedly favorable to a speedy restoration of the old schedule and a happy termination of this unfortunate strife.   JOHN H. PIERCE,
                                                                                    Editor.
Extract from editorial leader in THE LABOR PROBLEM of Minneapolis and St. Paul.

Remember Labor's May Day, Lyceum Theatre, Minneapolis,
MAY 1, 1894.

Union organizers like Eugene Debs, far left, gave speeches, wrote newspaper articles, held meetings, and talked to railway workers. They organized rallies like the one advertised in the poster. They used strong language, accusing company owners of cruel and selfish actions.

149

On April 18, 1894, Eugene Debs arrives in St. Paul and moves into the Sherman Hotel. He writes a note to Hill suggesting they meet to discuss the strike and settle their disgreement. He has terms by which the Great Northern Railway employees will return to work:

1. *Wages will be increased to their level before the first pay cut in August 1893.*

2. *If it is necessary for the railroad to cut costs, working hours will be shortened instead of firing employees.*

3. *There will be no prejudice against any employee who took part in the strike. Everyone will return to work and have an equal chance at promotion and a pay raise.*

4. *The new pay raise will start as soon as the employees go back to work.*

On April 19, 1894, Hill and Debs send letters to each other by messenger. They try to arrange a meeting but cannot agree on who should attend.

To Mr. Eugene Debs:

I am pleased you want to meet today. Our company is always ready to meet and hear from its employees on any topic. I want to remind you that we will meet only with the men on our payroll or with their representatives.

Yours truly,
James J. Hill

To Mr. James J. Hill:

If I understand your letter, you do not consider the men on strike as your employees. In that case, our committee cannot meet with you.

Yours very truly,
Eugene Debs

The Minneapolis Tribune reported that many people in towns along the Great Northern supported the strike. The townspeople shared the point of view of the union members.

Minneapolis Tribune.

MINNEAPOLIS, MINN., TUESDAY MORNING, APRIL 17, 1894.   PRICE: FIVE CENTS.

A VICTORY FOR REED

DEMOCRATS O. K. HIS QUORUM-COUNTING SCHEME.

Mills May Get It.

The Bourbon Members of the House Committee on Rules Agree to Report to the House Today a Rule Which Embodies the Plan Pursued by the Maine ... an When He Occupied the Chair Crisp Now Fills.

WASHINGTON, D. C., April 16.—After a session of two hours today, the Democratic members of the house committee on rules agreed on the new quorum-counting rule and then sent for Messrs. Reed and Burrows, the Republican members of the committee. It is understood that the rule provides for ascertaining a quorum by counting members present and not voting and also for fining members who absent themselves from the house. The new rule will probably be presented to the house tomorrow.

THE LAST OF EARTH.

Congress Does Honor to the Memory of the Late Senator Vance.

WASHINGTON, D. C., April 16.—When the senate reconvened at 3:30 o'clock this afternoon, after the recess taken out of respect to the late Senator Vance, the chamber presented a metamorphozed appearance. The chairs of the senators had been crowded more closely together, and additional seating capacity was obtained by bringing in a large number of folding chairs and placing them in every possible space. Large upholstered arm chairs were placed in the semi-circular space facing the vice-president's dais, those of the family of the deceased statesman and invited guests being on his left, and for the president and other officials on the right. On the clerk's desk was a massive floral piece, representing a tall column composed of dark corner colored leaves of the smilx, a

passed through Washington today for a two months' trip to Ireland. He has recently been employed on Vanderbilt's palace in North Carolina.

Maj. George Beardsley, Fargo, who has been spending the winter in the South and Washington, starts for home tomorrow.

WASHINGTON, D. C., April 16.—There is already more or less talk in the senate as to Senator Vance's successor on the finance committee. Conversations with a number of Democratic senators today develops the fact that a number of them are confident that the choice will fall on Senator Mills, of Texas.

Adverse to Kyle.

WASHINGTON, D. C., April 16.—The senate committee on public lands decided today to report adversely the amendment to the sundry civil bill proposed by Senator Kyle, providing that the act repealing the timber culture law shall not affect a contest pending in the land office prior to the passage of that act.

A Pardon by Grover.

WASHINGTON, D. C., April 16.—The president has pardoned John Lutz, sentenced in Utah to six years' imprisonment for adultery, finding that there is reason to believe that he was convicted upon false testimony.

Prohibition Case.

WASHINGTON, D. C., April 16.—In the supreme court today the prohibition case from North Dakota was set for the third Monday in October.

ENGAGED.

Announcement of the Betrothal of Miss Ethel Ingalls, Daughter of Ex-Senator John J. Ingalls.

ATCHISON, Kan., April 16.—The engagement is announced of Miss Ethel Ingalls to Dr. Edward G. Blair, of this city. Miss Ingalls is the oldest daughter of ex-Senator J. J. Ingalls and was for several years a reigning belle in Washington society. She has achieved some prominence as a writer.

THE GREAT NORTHERN STRIKE

STANDSTILL.

At Midnight Last Night the Strike Was on in Minnesota.

Over Two Hundred Employes Meet at St. Cloud and Vote to Join the Strikers.

Policemen Appointed From Their Ranks to Care for the Company's Property.

Cities All Along the Line Sympathize With the Men in Their Battle for Wages.

The Tie-Up Is Now Practically Complete From St. Paul to the Pacific Coast.

lowing resolutions were unanimously adopted:

Whereas, a strike has taken place on the Great Northern railroad, be it

Resolved, That the citizens of Havre, in sympathy with the employes of the Great Northern Railroad Company in this their movement; that the quiet and peaceable manner in which their movements have and are being conducted is fully indorsed and we earnestly hope for a speedy adjustment between employes and employers on a fair and equitable basis.

AT GREAT FALLS.

No Change in the Situation Is Noted in Montana.

Special Telegram to the Tribune.

HELENA, Mont., April 16.—There is no change here in regard to the Great Northern strike and no steps are expected to be taken looking to an adjustment of affairs until General Superintendent Bryan reaches St. Paul. He left here Sunday over the Northern Pacific and should reach St. Paul tomorrow, when the situation will be reported to President Hill. Strikers wish it understood that this affair was inaugurated and is being carried on by the American Railway Union. The Brotherhood of Locomotive Engineers takes no part. Jerry Derrigan, of the Great Falls division of the engineers' brotherhood, received a dispatch from J. C. Nolan at St. Paul, saying:

"Instruct our members to take no hasty action or go into any illegal strike, as they will positively get no support from the Brotherhood. Stand by your obligations and agreement, as you will be sufferers if you don't."

To this Mr. Derrigan replied: "Hands off. Great Northern engineers are acting under instructions of the American Railway Union. Every engineer to a man is

ALL READY.

Employes at Minneapolis Vote to Strike if They Are Ordered.

An Address by Vice-President Howard, of the American Railway Union.

The Trouble Seems to Be Caused by a War Between the Organizations.

Representatives of the Brotherhoods Meet President Hill and Mr. Case.

An Attempt Will Be Made in St. Paul Today to Fill Up the Breaches.

Would You Join the Strike?

Just think of what is happening! Hundreds of employees have walked off their jobs. They have left the trains in depots and railroad yards. Passengers and freight are stranded. Do you think the workers have a right to do that? Do you think Hill should agree to meet with Debs and his committee?

Imagine yourself in James J. Hill's shoes. Think of things from his point of view. He wants to keep his business going. He could replace the striking workers with others willing to work. What would you do in his place?

Now try to put yourself in the boots of someone who worked for the Great Northern Railway in 1894. Think of things from that point of view. Would you join the strike? How would you act?

On April 23, 1894, the governor of Minnesota tries to convince Hill and Debs to settle the strike. He writes a letter to both men:

Dear Sirs:

For several days a strike on the Great Northern Railway has interfered with travel and business. Many citizens of the state have asked me to help solve the problem. It is my duty to ask both of you to find a way to end the strike. Is it possible to settle this disagreement soon and avoid further loss to the public?

Knute Nelson
Governor of Minnesota

This coded telegraph message was sent to Hill from a business partner in New York. Other railroad companies, it says, will do whatever is necessary to help Hill fight the American Railway Union. Most railroad owners shared Hill's point of view.

Governor Knute Nelson

151

The strike is big news from St. Paul to Seattle. It's in all the newspapers. Everyone who works for the Great Northern Railway—and almost everyone who lives along its tracks—takes sides with Hill or Debs. People with different points of view write letters to Hill.

April 26, 1894
To James J. Hill:
Business owners here in Butte, Montana, support the strikers. They agree that wages are too low.

They will send a letter to the President of the United States today, asking him to help end the strike. Businesses here are closing because the freight trains have stopped.
W. W. Tilley

April 27, 1894
My Dear Mr. Hill:
You have gone as far as anyone could ask to solve this problem. It is too bad there is not wisdom and good judgment among your men.

You have been very fair and reasonable. Their failure to accept your offer has weakened them and strengthened you.
W. H. Nuesdale, Manager
M & St. L Railway

April 28, 1894
My Dear Sir:
I can run a handcar and work on the track here or any ordinary labor on the railroad. I can organize the farmers between Grand Forks and Fargo to look after your

Charles Pillsbury headed the committee that heard Hill and Debs describe the issues causing the strike. Hill expected the business owners to share his point of view and force the union members back to work.

track and cut the weeds for less than you are paying for it now and they will be almighty glad to get the money.

Budd Reeve
North Dakota Farmer

Two days later, a group of Minneapolis and St. Paul business owners invite Hill and Debs to discuss the strike at a meeting with them. Both Hill and Debs attend the meeting and give speeches. After their meeting, the business owners write a letter to Hill and Debs:

It is our opinion that the company and the union should agree to have the strike settled by a committee. The committee will consider all points of view and offer a plan to end the strike. Whatever wrongs exist should be righted. Justice should be found. At present, innocent people are suffering because the railway is not operating.

Hill and Debs agree to the plan. Hill believes the business owners agree with his point of view and will force Debs to end the strike. Debs believes the strength of his one big union will force the business owners to support his demands.

A committee of 14 business owners is appointed. On May 1, they meet to hear Hill and Debs discuss the strike again. The committee members review all the information and consider each point of view. They know that their conclusion will affect hundreds of railroad workers. It could mean the difference between profit and loss for the railroad.

Employees of the Hormel Company in Austin went on strike in 1933. The men and women interrupted work and blocked the entrance to the Hormel plant. Another strike at the plant made headlines in 1985 and 1986.

How Does the Strike End?

You have heard about the strike from several points of view. James J. Hill, Eugene Debs, the governor of Minnesota, men and women who live along the Great Northern tracks, and others affected by the strike have given you their opinions.

It's time now for *you* to settle the strike. You may support James J. Hill and his point of view. You may agree with Eugene Debs and support his union members. Or you may be a member of the committee selected to end the strike.

Divide your class into three groups. One group represents James J. Hill. Its members give speeches supporting his point of view. They may tell the committee that this strike is unfair because the employees quit with almost no notice and left trains, passengers, and freight stranded.

The second group represents Eugene Debs and the American Railway Union. Its members may give speeches supporting the union's demands.

A third group represents the committee of business owners appointed to end the strike. Its members will listen to all the speeches. Then, just like the original committee, they will write a plan to settle the strike. They must decide what is right and wrong.

Streetcar operators in St. Paul went on strike in November 1917. The Twin City Rapid Transit Company threatened to fire employees for wearing union buttons while driving the streetcars. Union members refused to take off the buttons. On November 23, the union president was fired for refusing to work overtime. Union members went on strike to protest. On November 28, they held a parade and demonstration in downtown St. Paul.

On May 1, 1894, the committee of 14 business owners met to write a report that would settle the strike. Their conclusions were based on the information you have read. Their point of view influenced their decision. They presented the report to Hill and Debs.

How did the members of your classroom committee settle the strike? Did they accept Hill's point of view? Did they accept the union's demands? Did they find a compromise? Your teacher will tell you how the strike was settled.

Compare your committee's decision with the settlement reached in 1894. Then you can decide whether the company or the union came out ahead and whether justice was served.

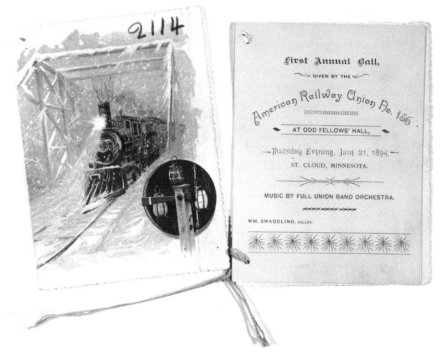

American Railway Union members held a party when the strike was settled. They hired a band, rented a hall in St. Cloud, and invited all their members. Do you think they had a reason to celebrate?

These women demonstrated support for the International Street Railway Trainmens Union on November 28, 1917.

For My
Valentine

Feb 14, '07

Although it was the day
after Valentine's we decided
to have our Valentine box
at the club and these
are some of the Valentines
I got. These are the home-
made ones and Linda

made up the verse in
hers.
    The club met over to
the Brights and first
we played a game. It
was that we either had
to write a poem on Lincoln
or Washington or make
a picture of them
two. Of course I got
a booby prize which is this

Linda gave me this

came the eatables and then
Valentine box. We had lots
Ruth and I whose
this month had caps
and the others different kinds

Linda's was
a big green
dunce cap

Activity 16
Some Things Don't Change

When you read a good story or watch a good movie you get interested right away. The action is exciting. The characters face challenges and experience emotions everyone recognizes. Love, fear, competition, jealousy, and selfishness are examples.

History describes the conflict and emotions of human experience, too. The difference is that history describes real events.

Dorothy Walton and Adina Adams were real people who faced problems and experienced emotions while they grew up in Minnesota. Dorothy and Adina were about your age in 1905. Neither of them became famous. Their

names and accomplishments aren't attached to important dates in history books. But both girls led lives full of events that were important to them.

Dorothy was born in Minneapolis. She grew up and went to school in a small neighborhood south of downtown. She had two sisters. Audrey was four years older than Dorothy. Grace was younger.

Adina Adams was born in St. Paul. She grew up in a house on St. Anthony Avenue. Her home and much of her old neighborhood are gone now. They were destroyed when Highway I-94 was built through the city.

Even though Dorothy was born almost a century ago, getting to

know her is easy. Dorothy wrote letters and saved the letters other people sent to her. She pasted photographs, concert tickets, and postcards in her scrapbook. She kept a record of her piano practice and of when she went to chorus. She made lists of her friends and the things they did together. Dorothy kept a record of almost everything she did.

Dorothy's scrapbooks, letters, and notes are primary sources of historical information. They tell where and when things happened, the problems she faced, and the emotions she felt. Just like a good story, her scrapbooks and letters describe experiences you can recognize.

Dorothy Walton celebrated Valentine's Day, Lincoln's birthday, and Washington's birthday all at once with a party on February 14, 1907. The eighth-grade girls made cards for each other, played games, had contests, ate candy and cookies, and laughed.

Dorothy's books are also evidence of her relationships with other people. They reveal her values, the things she felt were important.

Dorothy began writing in her diary when she was in grade school. She wrote letters and notes almost every day. Here's what she wrote on the first day of school after Christmas vacation:

Tuesday, January 2, 1906
Foggy and snowy. Woke up feeling as tired as when I went to bed at night. *Had a good breakfast. Went to school. Hate Miss Hunter worse than ever. After school we went sliding and had a fine time.*

Dorothy's diary wasn't fancy. Her notes each day were short. Here's another one:

Tuesday, February 6, 1906
Not so cold. The teacher told me that I wasn't very well prepared for seventh grade. I knew it. After school we went sliding in front of Maude's. I went down the hill over the drift and into the fence around the tennis grounds. I got a black eye, skinned my shin and eyebrow and knee.

You may recognize the feelings and events that Dorothy describes. Even though she lived far from you and a long time ago, you may have some things in common. As you read, keep track of the experiences you share with her.

PEEKING OVER THE ROOF

A PROFILE OF "YOURS TRULY"

PEEK A BOO

Does your family keep a scrapbook of snapshots like these of Dorothy Walton and her friends? Have you seen photographs of your parents or grandparents when they were your age?

Some pictures of the club

Summer of 1906.

Ma

Linda in her Sunday clothes

Asgers at the bonfire toasting marshmallows

"Willy" Linda's bird

Finding Similarities

Dorothy was excited about graduating from eighth grade. She wrote about some of the special events at the end of the school year. Here's how she described two of them:

June 6, 1907

We went to Excelsior on our school picnic today and had a dandy time. Linda and I shooted the shoots on our feet. That's like walking down a ladder. We had a PEACHY day and roller-skated till we went, which was at four.

July 5, 1907

We had the afternoon off because diploma day was this morning. So Agnes Potter and I made a cake for Miss Forester, who is getting married. The cake was half yellow and half white with a sunflower made of yellow and white candles for Douglas School colors in the center.

Dorothy wrote about things other than school. During the summer she spent time with friends and enjoyed her vacation. They had picnics, mowed the lawn, went to the lake, and stayed overnight with friends.

In 1907, Dorothy was 13. She started high school in September. The year turned out to be busy.

September 4, 1907

We started school today at East Side High. K and I went up alone

How will you feel on graduation day? How about the first day of high school? These pages from Dorothy's scrapbook give you an idea of how she felt on those days.

but were met by Mrs. Potter and Agnes. Mrs. Potter introduced Muriel, K, Agnes, and me to Mr. Webster and our teachers. We all sat together.

February 1, 1908

This morning Linda asked me to bring my sled, skis, and skates and spend the day with her. Talk about fun.

I got there just about lunch time. Linny made me the cutest cookies—hearts with arrows through them.

We had a dandy lunch. After lunch we went skiing over in the hollow. There was a path made there with a bump attached to it. You ought to have seen us go down that thing the first few times. I simply screamed at Linda.

I went down several times without falling, but poor Linny. She almost killed herself. We didn't stay out much more than half an hour as it was awfully cold and our feet nearly froze.

March 26, 1908

Stayed home from school. My throat hurt to swallow. Dad called in Doctor Law. *Scarlet Fever! Horrors!!!*

Dorothy's friends wrote letters to her while she was sick and stayed at home. Muriel, Linda, Agnes Bright, Agnes Potter, Katherine, and others wrote to tell her about gym class, chorus, club meetings, and each other. Katherine wrote about an argument she had with Agnes:

Dorothy was a freshman in high school when she put these photographs in her scrapbook. She wrote about skiing near her home and about a weekend with friends at Lake Minnetonka.

April, 1908

Oh, Tom! I'm mad. Agnes saw me writing a note to you while she was giving her book report and she took it and read it. I tried to take it away from her and she tore it. I hope Agnes has to recite and I'll get her so fussed she won't know what to do. Miss D. just told Juliet and me to stop whispering.

Your friend, K.

By May, Dorothy was back at school. It was difficult to make up the work she missed. She was disappointed with her grades. "I'm very much ashamed of this card," she wrote. "It might have been better if I hadn't had scarlet fever as I had such a lot to make up."

In 1910 Dorothy took a long trip out west with her father. Before she left, her friend Linda wrote a long letter to her. It included a list of things they had enjoyed together. Linda told Dorothy to think of them during her trip. The list includes events Dorothy described in her memory books.

After reading the letter, write three paragraphs. In the first paragraph, tell about an event or feeling in your life similar to one in Dorothy's. In the second paragraph, write about Dorothy's personality and the things she liked to do. In the third paragraph, describe Dorothy's relationships with the other people. What seemed to be important to her?

January 15, 1910
Dearest Tommy,
   I am going to give you a list of things to think of while you are gone.
1. Think of my fifth birthday party to which you came with long curls hanging down your back—at which time I was introduced to one of the dandiest girls I know.
2. Then think of the time when I dared you to go on some rubber ice and you fell in and were sent to Miss Forester's office.
3. Now remember the first day at high school.
4. Don't forget the house party and how we dressed up in each other's clothes.
5. Don't forget the night you stayed all night at my house and we climbed out on the roof.
6. Now think of Miss West's house party, about the ginger ale, and how unearthly early Miss West got up next morning.
7. Remember the day you and K and I went sliding on the big hill.
8. Think about the day we walked to St. Paul.
9. Now don't forget your old chum and don't forget to write soon.

   I hope you have a perfectly splendid trip.

   Linda

Dorothy invited some friends for a "pigtail party" at her house. The girls stayed overnight. They had pillow fights, turned somersaults on the bed, played games in the yard, took pictures like the one at left, and stayed awake until 3:00 A.M.

There's Less Information about Adina

Adina Adams didn't keep a scrapbook or a diary. She didn't save her letters. Most of her photographs were given away. Her report cards were lost.

Adina's family is listed in the 1900 census. It shows them living at 527 St. Anthony Avenue in St. Paul.

Adina's father, John Quincy Adams, was a newspaper editor. His paper, *The Appeal,* was well known. Adams wrote a story for his newspaper about Adina's tenth birthday party. The story appeared on May 30, 1904:

Sixty of the brightest girls and boys that could be found anywhere, all decked out in holiday attire, filled the home of Adina Adams last Saturday afternoon from 3 until 8 o'clock. When the guests had gathered, a piano solo was played by Gertrude Howard.

Then followed a little program: a piano solo by Ethel May Howard, piano solo by Roy Roberts, song "My Country Tis of Thee" *by everybody, and more.*

Then followed a number of games including bean bag and the heart game. Then came the peanut hunt. Refreshments were served at two tables, each set for 30 guests. The children all received a bag containing prizes. Later the children enjoyed lawn games. The gifts were most dainty and beautiful.

Old record books are the only evidence of Adina's school work. They show that she went to

Adina and her sisters posed for this photograph when they were teenagers. Adina is on the left. Margaret is in the middle. Edythella is on the right. Adina didn't save a scrapbook. This is the only picture we could find of her.

McKinley Grade School and then to Mechanic Arts High School. She was a student at Mechanic Arts from September 1908 to January 1909. She took algebra, history, English, Latin, mechanical drawing, and art.

On October 28, 1909, Minneapolis West High School played a football game against St. Paul Mechanic Arts. West was a brand new school and Dorothy was a tenth-grader there. Dorothy went to the game. She and Adina might have been sitting on opposite sides of the field cheering for different teams. (By the way, Mechanic Arts won the game, 12 to 0. "Poor West," said Dorothy. "Those boys were really rough.")

In 1970, the Minnesota Historical Society asked Adina to record some memories of her family. Adina was 76 years old when she told these stories about growing up in St. Paul:

We lived about two miles from downtown. My father took us everywhere and did everything for us. We had a lot of things like music lessons. We all learned to play the piano, except John. John was given a violin. My father had a wonderful library for us. We had hundreds of books. My father was a man that wanted his children to be well educated.

My sister Margaret passed away when she was 18. She was the most beautiful girl. Her beauty was in her character. She had beautiful eyes that sparkled. She was always head of her class. She wrote stories.

Dorothy's father, John Quincy Adams

Adina had some favorite memories of her family's home at 527 St. Anthony Avenue in St. Paul. This photograph appeared in her father's newspaper, The Appeal, *on September 24, 1910.*

She wrote poems. She was fun-loving. She could just do anything. We used to get a book a day from the library.

I remember when mother and we children went to a party at the home of the Hazel family. They lived in St. Anthony Park. It was near the railroad tracks. We were told from the very beginning that we mustn't go down by the railroad tracks. Of course children were attracted to the railroad tracks. The Hazel children, they knew better than to go beyond a certain point. But when nobody was looking, I went down to the tracks. Oh, boy, did I get it for doing that.

Even though Dorothy and Adina grew up in different cities and went to different schools, there were some important things they had in common. Think about the events in their lives and the things they seemed to value. Write one more paragraph about what Dorothy and Adina had in common.

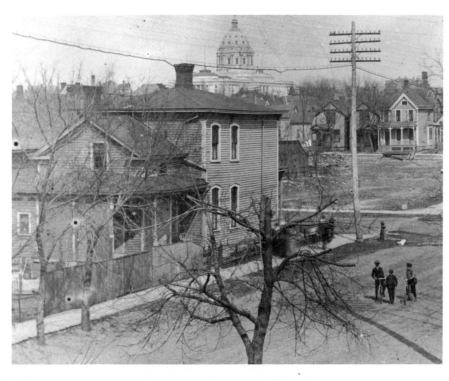

Adina's home was near the corner of Aurora and St. Anthony avenues, shown in 1907.

When I was 14, boys were still new to me. I hadn't paid any attention to them. But I remember Frank Wheaton. I was kind of sweet on him. I thought he was the cutest thing. At any rate, when Valentine's Day came, I received a big valentine. I was so excited about it. It had a Minneapolis postmark and of course I thought of Frank Wheaton because they lived in Minneapolis. I was thrilled about it.

There was a party given and my mother let me go. I went to the party and there was Frank. I waited for him to say something to me. Of course he moved around with all the girls. He was having a grand time. He didn't say anything to me.

My husband, who wasn't my husband then, and who I didn't pay any attention to, came over and sat down next to me. We were just watching the other kids dance. His name was Jasper Gibbs. We talked and talked, and finally I decided to ask him if he knew who sent that valentine. So I asked him if he knew.

He said, "Was it pretty?"
I said, "Yes."
He said, "Do you like it?"
I said, "Yes. Do you know?"
"Yes," he said.
"Well, why don't you tell me?"
"Well, I don't know whether I should or not."

He just wouldn't tell me. So finally I cornered his brother and I said, "Do you know who sent me this valentine?" And he said, "Why don't you ask Jasper?"

—From an interview with Adina Adams

Don't Lose Your History

Dorothy's memory book is a wonderful record of the past. She kept her diary and wrote letters to her friends and family for many years.

Adina's interview for the Minnesota Historical Society is full of good stories and information. But Adina's memory is incomplete. Many of the everyday events and emotions of her life have been lost.

Don't lose your history. Start your own scrapbook. It can be any size or shape. It doesn't have to be fancy. You can write in it, draw in it, or collect things in it. (Dorothy did all three.) The important thing is to enjoy using it and to use it often. A century from now, it may make you a famous person, too.

Adina may be in this picture of students at McKinley Elementary School.

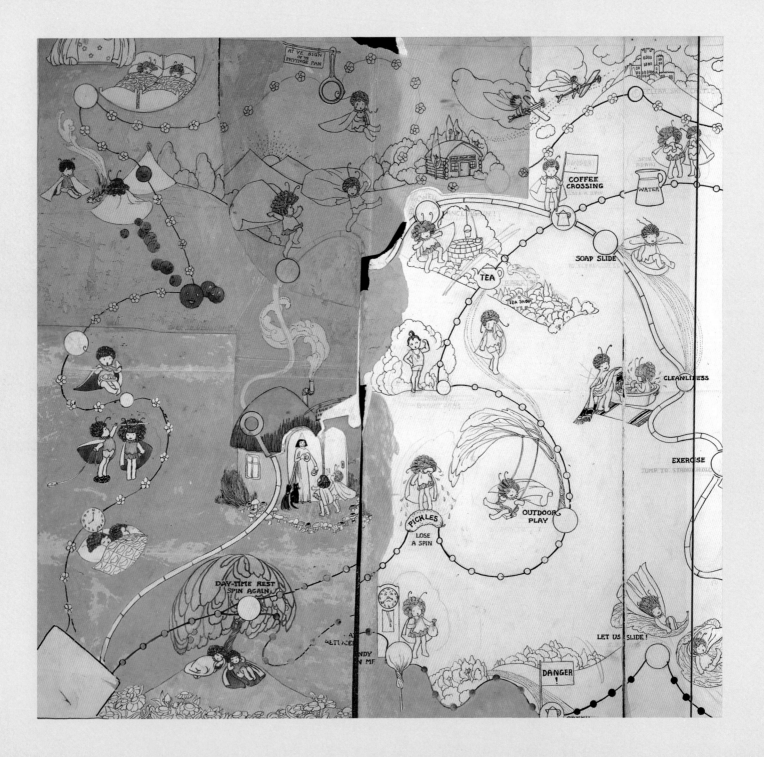

Activity 17
Writing from Minnesota

When I was ten years old and in fifth grade, I decided to write a novel. I had read several novels by then. My favorites were adventure stories written by Howard Pease. I thought writing a novel would be as much fun as reading one. I started work on a Saturday morning.

I knew I would need an office and thought my bedroom would do just fine. I moved my bed up against the wall. I pulled my desk—one of those old school desks with a drawer under the seat and a table top across the front—out from behind the door. I set up a card table and arranged on it paper, pencils, and an eraser. I carried my father's typewriter into my room and put it on the desk. I went to the kitchen, poured myself a very large glass of orange juice, and took it back to my new office. I closed the door, sat down, and started to type. I still remember my first sentence: "When Tim Taylor walked on board a tramp steamer headed for the south seas, he had no idea of the danger he would face before returning to San Francisco."

On Monday while I was at school, my mother turned my office back into a bedroom. She took down the card table, moved my desk back behind the door, returned my father's typewriter, and pulled my bed away from the wall. That was nearly 40 years ago. I still haven't finished that novel.

Other writers have been more successful. They write interesting and entertaining stories. They cleverly present the characters and plot. They skillfully describe events. The best writers—as well as artists who paint, dance, perform, design, or build something—find just the right word, sound, movement, or color to express their ideas. That's not easy to do. It takes practice, hard work, and talent.

Wanda Gág at her home in New Ulm in 1914. She was 20 years old.

Wanda Gág and a friend made up this game when they were children. There were rules, dice, game pieces, and a board. Wanda turned the game board into a work of art. She drew a design with ink and started to paint, but she never finished the project.

Wanda Gág

Wanda Gág (Gog) got her start as an artist in Minnesota. She was born in 1893 and grew up in New Ulm. In grade school, she began drawing pictures to go with the poems and stories she wrote. She sent her work to the *Minneapolis Journal*. The newspaper published her work in a special section called the *Journal Junior*. They paid her for the work, too.

Wanda was 15 years old in October 1908 when she began keeping a diary. She wrote about her friends and family, the events in her life, and her ideas about art.

From *Growing Pains: Diaries and Drawings for the Years 1908–1917* by Wanda Gág, first published in 1940:

One day, I came across an old half empty ledger of my father's. In our household, anything which could be drawn or written upon was in great demand; a notebook of any kind was a positive treasure. I began recording my earnings and expenditures, what drawings I had sent where and when, and other notes. I was never able to limit myself to plain figures and facts; so reports on the weather, family incidents, even youthful thoughts and yearnings, found their way into my writing.

May 21, 1909
My head is so full of new ideas that I've got the beginnings of a great many and the ends of hardly

Wanda made this drawing for her book, Gone is Gone.

Wanda drew these cartoons with pen and ink. The drawings belong to the Children's Literature Research Collection at the University of Minnesota in Minneapolis.

any! They whirl around at a great rate with no destination. Oh I wish I wouldn't have to work and go to school for a day or two so I could sketch and draw and paint, and paint and draw and sketch.

August 14, 1910
When I read stories about artists I get to thinking about art more than ever. It seems that everyone who is an artist, or hopes to be one (as it is in my case) has a style of their own. Just think of all the artists waiting to become famous.

Where will they find enough individuality in their work? I'm sure I don't know, but I suppose they will when the time comes.

December 3, 1910
People positively don't understand me. They even tell me to stop drawing and painting altogether. Goodness knows I couldn't, and if I could, I shouldn't, I'm too much in love with art for that. I can't help it that I've got to draw and paint forever; I cannot stop. I <u>cannot</u>, CANNOT!

Wanda left New Ulm in 1917. She moved to Minneapolis to attend art school. Three years later, she won a scholarship to study art in New York City. Her drawings became popular. In 1928 she was asked by an editor at a publishing company to write and illustrate a book for children. Wanda was thrilled. She wrote and illustrated *Millions of Cats*. The book was published in September 1928. It became one of the most famous of all children's books.

Wanda Gág wrote nine more books for children. She continued to draw and paint and to show her work in art galleries. In 1940, she published her diaries as a book called *Growing Pains*. Wanda died of cancer in 1945. Her drawings and manuscripts were collected and saved. Most of her work—all of the drawings, poems, and stories in this book—are kept at the University of Minnesota's Walter Library in the Children's Literature Research Collection.

Wanda was 20 years old when she designed the poster above for a national contest. At left, Wanda sketches a portrait of her sister, Stella.

F. Scott Fitzgerald

About the time Wanda Gág was writing and drawing for the *Journal Junior,* Scott Fitzgerald was writing stories for his school magazine. During the 1920s and 1930s, he became one of the most popular writers in America. In 1920, he wrote about himself and his art in an article for the *Saturday Evening Post:*

When I lived in St. Paul and was about 12, I wrote all through every class in school in the back of my geography book and first-year Latin book and in the margins of themes and mathematics problems. Two years later my family decided that the only way to force me to study was to send me to boarding school. That was a mistake. It took my mind off my writing.

In 1910, while he was 13, Scott wrote a short story called "Reade, Substitute Right Half." Like Wanda Gág's diary, it shows how he practiced writing.

"Hold! Hold! Hold!" the slogan thundered up the field to where the battered Crimson Warriors trotted wearily into their places again. The Blues attack this time came straight at center and was good for a gain of seven yards. "Second down, three," yelled the referee, and again the attack came straight at center. This time there was no withstanding the rush and the huge Hilton fullback crushed through the Crimson line again and shaking off his many tacklers, staggered on toward the Warrentown goal.

Scott Fitzgerald published sports stories and mysteries in the school magazine above, when he was a student at St. Paul Academy. In 1910 he performed in a recital at Professor Baker's Dancing School. He stands in the back row, far right.

The teams sprang into line again, but Hearst, the Crimson right tackle, lay still upon the ground. The right halfback was shifted to tackle and Berl, the captain, trotted over to the sidelines to ask the advice of the coaches.

"Who have we got for halfback, sir?"

"Suppose you try Reade," answered the coach. "That's all we have."

"I guess he'll do," said Berl.

"Come on kid," and they trotted onto the field.

In the game's next few minutes, Reade made an important tackle, recovered a fumble, and carried the ball several times for Warrentown. Nevertheless, the Hilton Blues threatened to score again and win the game:

When the Blues were on the Crimson's ten-yard line, their quarterback made his only error. He gave the signal for a forward pass. The ball was shot to the fullback, who turned to throw it to the halfback. As the pigskin left his hand, Reade

leaped upward and caught the ball. He stumbled for a moment, but, soon getting his balance, started out for the Hilton goal with a long string of Crimson and Blue men spread out behind him. He had a start of about five yards on his nearest opponent, but this distance was decreased to three before he had passed his own 45-yard line. He turned his head and looked back. His pursuer was breathing heavily and Reade saw what was coming. He was going to try a div-

F. Scott Fitzgerald at 15

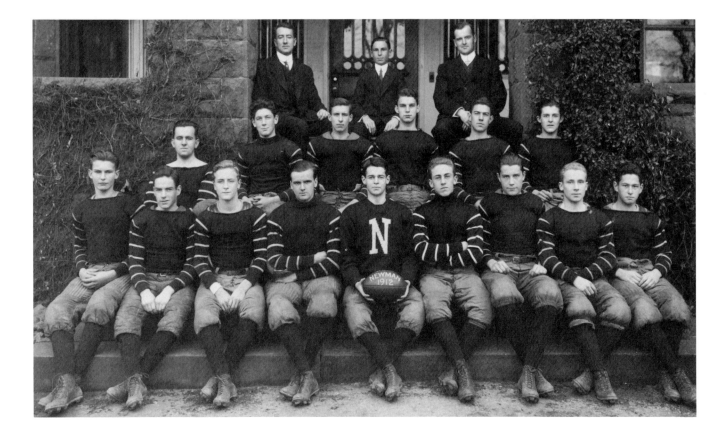

Fitzgerald is pictured here with his Newman School football team in 1912. He is seated in the front row, third from the left.

Scott went to boarding school in 1911. He liked to play football and write stories. He wrote poetry, too. After one of his football games, he wrote a long poem. Here are some lines:

Watch that line, now crouching
    waiting,
In their jersies white and black;
Now they're off and charging, making
Passage for the plunging back.
Buck your fiercest, run your fastest,
Let the straight arm do the rest.

171

ing tackle. As the man's body shot out straight for him, Reade stepped out of the way and the man fell harmlessly past him, missing him by a foot.

From there to the goal line it was easy running, and as Reade laid the pigskin on the ground and rolled happily over beside it he could just hear another slogan echo down the field: "Reade! Reade! Reade!"

Scott wrote his first novel, *This Side of Paradise,* while he lived in an apartment on Summit Avenue in St. Paul. He was only 23 years old. He wrote short stories for popular magazines like *Esquire* and *Saturday Evening Post.* Some of his stories are based on his experiences growing up in St. Paul. His most famous novel is *The Great Gatsby.*

Scott Fitzgerald wrote most of his stories, novels, movie scripts, and essays during the 1920s and 1930s. He kept a journal, too. Some say he could describe those times and the people who lived through them better than any other writer in America. Fitzgerald didn't have a very long career. He died of a heart attack when he was just 44 years old.

Fitzgerald's novel, This Side of Paradise, *was published when he was just 23 years old. He wrote four other novels:* The Last Tycoon, Tender is the Night, The Beautiful and the Damned, *and* The Great Gatsby. *He wrote more than 150 short stories and published more than 35 essays in books and magazines.*

Gordon Parks

Gordon Parks came to Minnesota from Kansas. His father was a farm worker there. His mother worked at home and cared for their 15 children. When she died in 1928, Gordon's father sent him to live with his sister and her husband in St. Paul. He was full of fear and sadness when he left Kansas. He was 16 years old. Later, he wrote about his first days in St. Paul in his book, *A Choice of Weapons*. First published in 1966, it describes his life from the time he left Kansas for St. Paul in 1928, until 1944:

I enrolled in Mechanic Arts High School, and got an evening job bussing dishes in a diner, where I was paid $6.00 a week and given one meal a day. My brother-in-law took $2.00 for my rent and meals, yet the $4.00 left were more than I had ever had at one time in my entire life.

Gordon didn't get along with his brother-in-law. They fought and he was thrown out of their house.

He was all alone. He had no place to live. He was black and poor and in a place where discrimination was common. He hung out in a pool hall on St. Anthony Avenue. He rode the bus at night back and forth between Minneapolis and St. Paul until morning when he could go back to school:

The harder times became, the more determined I was to stay in school. The necessity of learning came with the first pangs of hunger, with the first homeless night.

Gordon Parks chose this photograph (and two others on page 175) from his personal collection for Northern Lights. *He made this photograph in 1970. It is called* Muslim Women.

Gordon's art is inspired by the events and people in his life. His music, photography, and writing describe his emotions and experience. One of his songs came from the sadness he felt after a quarrel with his girlfriend, Sally Alvis. The song he wrote was called "No Love." He was just 19 years old. A year later, while he was working as a busboy at the Hotel Lowry in St. Paul, he got a lucky break:

Each day after they served lunch, I had the main dining room and the huge grand piano all to myself. Once the tables were set for the evening, I played away. One afternoon I was playing and singing "No Love" when I felt someone was behind me. It was Larry Duncan, the orchestra leader.

"Is that your music?" he asked.

"Yes."

"Would you like to have our orchestra play your song?"

"I sure would," I said, and it was probably the understatement of my lifetime. The orchestra arranger spent the rest of that afternoon with me, taking the piece down as I played it.

On Friday night, Larry motioned me toward the bandstand. "We're broadcasting 'No Love' on the network tomorrow night—with your permission, of course," he said. On the night of the broadcast, Abby, the drummer, showed a group of waiters and myself the program.

There was my name among those of Irving Berlin, Duke Ellington, Cole Porter, and Jerome Kern. When at last the moment came, just before the vocalist approached the microphone, I stood near the bandstand where I could hear him sing my lyrics.

When the orchestra finished, I telephoned Sally. "Yes, I listened," she said. "It was beautiful."

Gordon Parks also used sculpture, short stories, poetry, and painting to express his ideas

Gordon Parks was talented and determined, and he survived. He learned to play the piano and compose music. He studied art and learned photography. He began to write and paint. His photography is now world famous. He has directed movies, written novels, poetry, movie scripts, and essays. He composes classical music and popular songs.

No Love

Now that you're gone nights are so long.
Days aren't what they used to be. Weeks linger on.
Everything's going wrong.
I'm lost until you return to me.

There's no love since you are gone, dear,
I'm lost. Let's make amends, sweetheart.
I'm lost when you're not near.
Please say you'll be back soon, sweetheart.
I dreamt you came back last night to me,
Came back in answer to my whispered plea.
But sweet dreams make me heartsore, dear.
I wake and you're not near,
So there's no love 'til you return to me.

and feelings. He began to think about the power of photography. He was impressed by a collection of photographs he saw in a magazine:

They were photographs of migrant workers. Dispossessed, beaten by dust storms and floods, they roamed the highways in caravans of battered jalopies and wagons between Oklahoma and California scrounging for work. The names of the photographers too stuck in my mind—Arthur Rothstein, Russell Lee, Dorthea Lange, and others. These stark images of men, women, and children saddened me. I took the magazine home and kept looking at those photographs for months.

He bought a used camera and started taking pictures. He got his first break as a photographer from Madeline Murphy, the owner of a fashionable store in St. Paul. He asked for a chance to photograph her merchandise. "I'm willing to give you a chance," she told him.

Gordon Parks made these photographs for different purposes. The photo at far left is Paris Fashion, taken in 1948, The photo at left is Poverty, Brazil. It was taken in 1961.

"I think it would be fun. Can you be here tomorrow evening, right after we close? I'll have the models and dresses ready."

"Oh sure. I'll be here right on the dot," he said.

His photograhy was imaginative. It made an impression. He was offered a job in Chicago, where his work became well known. In 1942, Gordon received a scholarship to work and study photography in Washington, D.C.

Gordon met other photographers in Washington whose work he admired. After his first assignment, his supervisor gave him some advice: "You can't just take a picture. You have to find logical ways to express your feelings and ideas. The right words, too, are important. They should underscore your photographs.

Think in terms of images and words. They can be mighty powerful when they are fitted together properly."

Gordon Parks's photography improved and his reputation grew. In 1949, he was offered a job with *Life* magazine. He worked for the magazine until 1972. His photographs and articles have been seen by millions of people around the world.

Minnesota has had other wonderful artists like Wanda Gág, Scott Fitzgerald, and Gordon Parks. Their work has influenced the way we think about ourselves and each other. Their art describes our values—the things we believe are important and good. It entertains us and gives us pleasure.

Libby Larsen grew up practicing the piano each morning before breakfast and sailing X-boats on Lake Harriet each weekend. She began writing music in seventh grade when she wrote her class song at Christ the King School in Minneapolis. Larsen was a serious composer while she was in high school. By the time she got to college, other musicians were interested in her music and wanted to perform it. That was exciting and encouraging.

Libby has become one of the finest composers in the United States. Her works are performed by symphony orchestras, soloists, and opera companies all over the country. She enjoys conducting orchestras and smaller groups performing her music.

Larsen continues to compose music at her home in Minneapolis and to perform in the United States, Canada, and Europe. "I've always been interested in sound more than other senses like sight or touch. Sound is all around us. Each of us composes in the way we order the sound around us."

It's a tradition in some families that young women learn the art of needle-work. Their first project is often a sampler. It's a pattern designed to teach them several stitches. There are letters, numbers, decorations, a border design, and usually a short verse to complete. When they finish, they are prepared to work on bigger, more complicated projects.

Here are directions for a special sampler. It's designed to introduce you to the way artists express ideas with images and words. It's a Minnesota sampler. It's part sculpture, part short story, part painting, and part puzzle. This is the way it works: Begin with five pieces of cardboard or construction paper. Each should be square, 10 inches on a side. Tape the pieces together according to the diagram below. Then fold them together and tape them to make a box. Your Minnesota sampler will be a cube with one side missing.

Your job is to fill each side—including the inside—with a different work of art. Each of your creations will have a specific subject. You may decide how to match the art with each topic. Here are the subjects you must use:

1. A place in Minnesota
2. A person you know
3. A trip to someplace in Minnesota
4. Someone in Minnesota's past
5. An event in Minnesota history
6. Yourself

Here are the art forms you must use:
1. A group of photographs
2. A very short story
3. A poem, song, or musical composition
4. A drawing or painting
5. A map or a puzzle
6. A sculpture

You may choose any of the six art forms for any one of your subjects. There are only three requirements:
1. You must use each art form.
2. You must present each topic.
3. You must use all five sides of the box—including the inside.

When you finish, hang your Minnesota sampler from the ceiling or mount it on a stand. Display it for others to enjoy and appreciate.

Put the sides of your sampler together like this . . .

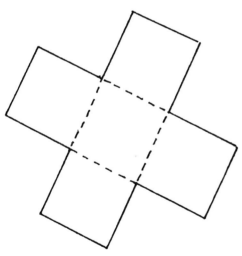

. . . so it looks like this.

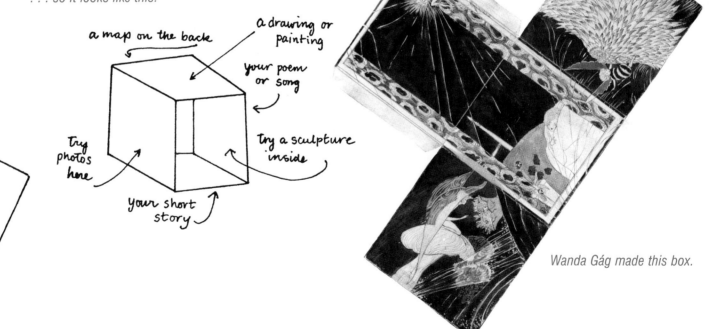

a map on the back

a drawing or painting

your poem or song

try a sculpture inside

try photos here

your short story

Wanda Gág made this box.

177

Activity 18
History Uncovered

Alice Nelson stood next to her sewing machine in the back bedroom of her farm home near Hanley Falls, Minnesota. She held a quilt folded in her arms. You could see the quilt's pattern of brightly colored fabric.

"I started my first quilt when I was just 12. That was in 1930. I needed help on that one. My mother worked with me to finish. We did the quilting together. I wasn't patient enough. She told me, 'Keep the stitches small. No one likes long stitches.' Finally, she sat down next to me and started stitching, and we worked together until it was done."

She laid the quilt on the top of the trunk in which it had been stored. She let one edge of the quilt fall to the floor. You could see the entire pattern of small fabric patches sewn into a colorful design. Nelson kept talking. "You can see where my mother worked.

Her stitches are smaller and more beautiful. I learned a lot from this one.

"I started my next quilt just before I graduated from high school. I didn't need any help on that one. I had the pattern and colors already picked out. It was the Irish Chain. Most of the fabric was leftover from other things I made. I bought some of the fabric in Marshall. The filling was wool. Most peole used cotton. Now some use a synthetic.

"It took all spring to cut the pieces and to sew them together. I could have used the sewing machine, but I did it by hand. We had a quilting frame set up in the spare bedroom. I had a templet to trace a pattern for the stitches. I had to keep making new templets—cutting them out of brown wrapping paper like paper snowflakes. Now you buy plastic templets that don't wear out.

These girls quilted in 1935 with scraps left from other sewing projects. They tied the quilt with bits of yarn to keep the lining in place.

Alice Nelson writes a little history with each quilt she sews. Quilts are unusual and valuable sources of history. Some are used as gifts that celebrate special events. Others are made only for warmth during cold winter nights. They are works of art often made from leftover fabric and assembled with patience, imagination, and skill.

"I finished that quilt during the summer. I don't know if it's my favorite, but it's the one with the most memories attached to it. My mother did a quilt when she was 17, too. I don't know what happened to that one."

Alice Nelson folded her quilt and put it back in the trunk. She pointed to the pieces of material on the table next to her sewing machine. "I've been working on this one for a month. I want to finish it before Christmas."

Nelson unfolded the fabric. "I'm making this one for my daughter. After I get it on the frame, the stitching should take about a month."

The quilt's cotton back was folded loosely on her ironing board. She unfolded the material and draped it over the quilting frame. She pinned one edge to the strip of cotton wrapped around one side of the frame. Then she pinned the second edge of the fabric to the opposite side of the

frame. She adjusted the end pieces of the frame and pinned one edge of the fabric to each. She loosened the clamps at each corner, stretched the material tight across the frame, and fastened the clamps again.

"I have about five pounds of cotton filling for this one. This quilt will be 96 inches long by 84 inches wide. You need about half a pound of batting per square yard." She unrolled the cotton across the stretched fabric, cut it to the

Alice Nelson pinned the patterned top of her quilt to the frame. She added the quilt's cotton backing and lining. She stretched each piece tight to avoid wrinkles.

proper length, and then put on a second layer, laying it down in the opposite direction.

She brought the patterned top from the table beside her sewing machine to the frame. "Look at the back of this spread. You have to press every seam flat before pinning it on the frame. Otherwise the seams will stretch unevenly, and the patches will pucker up." She laid the fabric carefully over the batting. She pinned it at the corners first. Then she put a pin

at the middle of each side. Gradually, she attached the whole piece of fabric to the frame.

Nelson brought a kitchen chair next to the quilting frame and sat down as if she were at the dinner table. She placed her templet on top of the quilt. She traced the templet with a pencil across one block of the quilt. She put the templet aside, took a small needle with white thread, and began stitching. She held the needle in her right hand while her left hand

supported the fabric. Her stitches were small—about 10 or 12 to an inch. It took half an hour to finish stitching the pattern on one block. She moved her chair slightly to the right, traced another pattern, and began stitching again.

The patchwork pattern was made from pieces of printed fabric, cut into small squares and triangles. The pieces were stitched together by hand to form baskets filled with flowers. The baskets were stitched to a white cotton

Alice used a special needle for stitching the design. Her favorite is a #10 quilting needle made in England. It is about 1⅛ inches long. The needles must be sharp to keep the stitches neat and crisp.

181

background. Nelson's stitching outlined each basket, then made a pattern around the baskets. The pattern is called Garden Basket.

The Garden Basket is a traditional pattern, sometimes used by farming families and often given from mother to daughter. Many patterns have names associated with special events. Album Patch, for example, is often used for friendship quilts given as farewell gifts or on special occasions. Friends make and sign individual quilt blocks—sometimes embroidered with short poems or sayings.

Some patterns and colors are traditional in certain parts of the country. Others are used most often by one group of people or another. Quilt patterns are often published in magazines. Others have been designed by one quilter and copied by others. Quilting is so individual. Women sew with fabric they used for a hundred different reasons. There is wide variety even in the most traditional patterns.

Alice Nelson gave this quilt to her daughter, Mary Taylor, in 1988. She used a traditional Garden Basket design found in a quilting book. She chose the pattern for her quilting stitches from another book.

Quilting Traditions

European settlers in America decorated quilts with designs cut from a popular cotton fabric made in England called chintz. The colorful chintz pieces were stitched onto a quilt top. The technique is called *appliqué,* and some people still make quilts that way.

American textile mills began making cotton fabric near the end of the 18th century. Women bought American cotton when it became less costly than material sent from Europe. They designed patterns with solid color patches left from other sewing. By 1860, cottons printed in bright designs by machines were available. Quilt patterns made with the new colorful fabrics (like Alice Nelson's Garden Basket) became popular.

Each block of this quilt represents a different Minnesota farm organization. It was used as the prize in a raffle. Each block was made from a design cut from fabric in a technique called appliqué.

Dolly Spencer and friends, quilting at a 1975 senior citizens' meeting in St. Paul

"The first quilts I remember are patchwork patterns, like this one," Nelson said, nodding toward the quilt stretched on her frame. "My mother made crazy quilts, too. So did others around here. They were made from different kinds of fabric—silk, wool, cotton, velvet, ribbon, almost anything. The pieces were sewn together in no special pattern. Sometimes women would sew the pieces together with an embroidery stitch. Crazy quilts take less time to make. The work isn't as fine. We used an old blanket instead of cotton for filling. The layers were tied together with yarn or thread, instead of quilted."

Quilters usually cut and sew the pattern pieces by themselves. Sometimes several women get together to help with the stitching. Alice Nelson says she usually does all the stitching by herself. "My mother and grandmother went to quilting bees, but they aren't so frequent any more. Quilting bees were social events, like a meeting to talk and get caught up. People get together in different ways now."

Like needlepoint samplers and embroidery, quilting has been done most often by women. Quilts are made by women living in cities, in small towns, and on farms. They are made by women of all ages, both rich and poor. Quilts have often become family treasures. They are valued for their usefulness, for sentimental reasons, and for their beauty. The patterns, colors, textures, and stitching in a quilt are as carefully chosen as the colors of a painting or the notes in a piece of music.

Cora Gray Brill made the silk, satin, and taffeta patchwork quilt at right in 1905. She sewed her initials and the date into the fabric. The border is black velvet with pink satin triangles. Cora stitched the pieces together with decorative embroidery. The back is a silk pattern of flowers in blue, green, and pink.

184

A Treasure Chest of History

Much of what we know about the past comes from documents and objects that describe the lives of wealthy and influential people. The information is more often about men than women. It tells the story of extraordinary events more often than common occurrences. Learning the history of ordinary people and everyday events is difficult. It takes imagination and hard work to find the right sources. It's like searching for treasure. That's why quilts are so important. They are a source of history that has often been overlooked.

Quilts are unusual historical sources. They aren't "written" in a language that is easily understood. They don't often include pictures of familiar places and people. Instead, quilts are stingy with their information. You have to collect and study many quilts to learn much history. The job takes time. It's worth the effort because no other sources have the same information about the women who made quilts and the people who used them.

Start your treasure hunt by looking for clues in just one quilt. Ask someone you know to bring a quilt to your classroom. Prepare for the visit by organizing some questions to ask about the quilt, its owner, and the person who made the quilt. (Remember, the information you discover in your research depends on the questions you ask and the care with which you study your source.)

Asian immigrants brought their history to Minnesota on quilts, too. Chia Yang began to sew as a child in Laos. By the time she was 10 years old, she had made a set of clothing and was a skilled artist. Chia's family was forced from its home by war in 1979. She was in a Thai refugee camp when an American volunteer encouraged her to sell some of her work in the United States. Her quilt patterns were made in bright colors using a reverse appliqué style. Some of the designs are traditional, others are her own invention. Chia's work became popular when it was sold at a St. Paul store called Hmong Handwork. In 1988, Chia and her family moved to Minnesota.

185

Be sure to handle the quilt with care. Put a careful person in charge of taking notes. Accuracy is important.

Start asking questions about the quilt. How long and wide is it? What is it made of? What pattern is used and why was it chosen? When was it made and where? Why was it made? (For a special occasion?)

Learn about the quilter. Who was she? What was her occupation? Was she married? Did she have children? Where did she live? Where was she born? Where were her parents born? What jobs did others in her family have? Did she make other quilts? What other patterns did she use? What happened to them? How were the quilts used?

Find out about the person who owns the quilt. Was the quilt a gift, or was it purchased? How is it used now?

Be sure to keep the owner's name, address, and telephone number. If you have a camera in class, take a picture of the quilt and its owner. Can you get a photograph of the person who made the quilt?

Your class may wish to examine more quilts. As your file of information grows, study it for clues to the lives of the women who made the quilts and the people who used them. What does your evidence tell you about the events they considered important? What does it tell you about their values? Does it give you a clue to how the lives of men and women may have been different? Does it give you ideas about how they spent their time? Does it suggest how the lives of people from different backgrounds may have been different?

If you can answer some of those questions, your project will be a success. It will uncover knowledge and information about people, events, and ideas often overlooked in history books.

Above are women at a quilting bee in 1895. The crazy quilt at right was made by Cordelia Teachout of Farmington when she was 70 years old. The quilt, of velvet, taffeta, and satin, has a ribbon from the 1885 state fair, sewn in as one of the patches.

People all over the country are interested in quilts for both their beauty and the history they tell. Some have organized groups to collect information about quilts. One group got started in Minnesota during 1986. It's called the Minnesota Quilt Project.

You can start a quilt project in your own neighborhood, town, or county. Invite quilt owners to your classroom. Examine the quilts and interview their owners. Take photographs of the quilts. Try to find photographs of the women who made them. Give each quilt a number. (You might make small patches with the name of your project and a number for the quilt. The patch could be sewn to the back of every quilt you examine.)

You might share your information with the Minnesota Quilt Project or compare it to the evidence collected by another class in another town or county.

Your class can add its own quilt to the project. Each of you can make one quilt square. Be sure to put your name or initials on your square. Sew them together and hang the patchwork fabric on the wall in your classroom. Choose one pattern for the quilt, or let students choose a pattern for their own squares. Be sure all the squares are the same size so they will fit together in a pattern.

When you finish, add the information about your quilt to the files of your documentation project. Take a picture of your class with its quilt. Have two copies of the picture made. Put one in a frame on the wall and the other in your files.

In 1885 these women quilted the Double Irish Chain, one of the most popular of all patterns. Look closely to see the ropes attached to each corner of the quilting frame. When work was not being done on the quilt, the frame was hoisted to the ceiling.

187

Activity 19
People Still Remember

Much of the world was tangled in war in 1944. Countries in Europe, North and South America, Asia, and Africa fought each other for land, power, and influence. Few people were untouched by the war.

Minnesota families struggled with the war, too. Henry Peterson was farming near Moorhead. His four brothers were in the service, and he was without the help needed to harvest. Boyd Wright was an army supply clerk assigned to a segregated unit stationed in North Africa. Marjorie Anderson lived in Minneapolis with her four-year-old son. Her husband was the captain of a patrol and torpedo boat fighting in the South Pacific. Joyce Yamamoto began her life in a detention camp for Japanese Americans in Arizona.

There are no books about Henry Peterson, Boyd Wright, Marjorie Anderson, or Joyce Yamamoto. The details of their lives during the war aren't recorded in diaries or letters. Their stories have survived, however. They have been saved as oral history.

Oral history is a recorded conversation with someone about their memories of the past. It is different from a diary or reminiscence because the interviewer directs the conversation with a series of questions. Oral histories may provide information that cannot be found in written sources or learned from objects.

Any topic may be the subject of an oral history. Two favorites are family and neighborhood history. Oral histories don't have to be about things that happened long ago. They may record information about recent events, too.

Some groups of people have always depended on oral histories to describe the past. Many American Indians have kept their history collected in stories told by one generation to another.

World War II caused a shortage of workers in many parts of the state. These women from Walker and Cass Lake traveled to southern Minnesota to help farmers detassel corn on July 20, 1943.

Posters, magazine ads, and billboards encouraged people to be patriotic during World War II. Your grandparents may remember posters like these. Ask them how the war affected their lives.

One Oral History Project

Almost everyone who lived through the years 1939 to 1945 remembers something about World War II. The interviews with Henry Peterson, Boyd Wright, Marjorie Anderson, and Joyce Yamamoto describe events that occurred during those years. Each person represents many others with similar experiences. In addition, each interview gives some hints about how to collect a good oral history.

The interview with Henry Peterson is a good example. He talks about German prisoners of war working on his farm near Moorhead in 1943 and 1944. The interviewer asks questions to learn details of the events. She does a good job of introducing herself, Peterson, and the topic of their conversation. The interview is hard to hear, however. (Imagine yourself listening to a tape recording as you read.) The speakers are sitting too far from the microphone. Their voices are faint and there is noise in the background. When you record an oral history, be sure to sit close to the microphone and speak up.

Today is Friday, January 11, 1973. I am Gloria Thompson, and I'm talking with Mr. Henry Peterson of Moorhead, Minnesota. Our topic is Mr. Peterson's experience farming during World War II.

Q: Mr. Peterson, you said there was a labor shortage during the war. How bad was the labor shortage?

Ask your parents and grandparents whether they knew German prisoners worked on Minnesota farms during World War II. These "POWs" worked near Moorhead, some of them on the Henry Peterson farm in 1943 and 1944.

A: *Very bad. That was the reason we used the prisoners. Four of my brothers were in the service. We didn't have enough help to plant or harvest.*

Q: *How did you find out that the army would let you use prisoners to work on your farm?*

A: *We read about it in the paper. We contacted the army and found out that some of the prisoners were sent to Minnesota. We could go to the camp and pick them up. Each crew had four prisoners and a guard.*

Q: *How long did they work each day?*

A: *Ten hours a day. We paid 40 cents an hour. The prisoners got 10 cents an hour and the rest went to the army.*

Q: *What had the prisoners done in the war?*

A: *Most of them had been foot soldiers. One group had been in Russia, close enough to see Moscow before they had to retreat. Others were fighting in North Africa. They didn't speak English well so it was difficult to find out details.*

Q: *What were your feelings about the prisoners?*

A: *A little hesitant. Later we got along with them just like other people. I remember one day their guard went to sleep. They just kept working.*

Q: *How did they act toward you?*

A: *At first they were cautious. They had been told not to talk. Later they didn't show any distrust.*

Henry R. Peterson

These German prisoners helped to build their prison camp near Moorhead. Farmers hired prisoners to paint buildings, pick rocks from their fields, operate machinery, and harvest crops.

Boyd A. Wright [signature]

The interview with Boyd Wright shows how follow-up questions may lead to very important information. The conversation began as a history of Wright's life. When he said, "I joined the army in 1941," the interviewer asked a follow-up question. The answer led to information about the segregation of black soldiers during World War II.

Q: What was the army experience like for blacks?

A: I had heard so much about the army, I thought that now I'm going to get a fair shake. I was never so disappointed. My brother and I were drafted. We went out to Fort Snelling. They lined us up and then sent off the white boys. Here we were still standing. So I asked Frank, "What's going on?" In the end we found out that all the boys from around here were going to the air corps. No place for Frank and me. They put us on a train to Leavenworth, Kansas.

Black men and women in the army during World War II served in segregated units. Some of these soldiers in basic training at Fort Wolter in Texas were sent from Minnesota on "colored only" railroad cars. They lived and worked separately from white soldiers. Many black units had black officers while stationed in the United States. Most had white officers when serving overseas.

Q: Was Leavenworth a segregated camp?

A: Well, Leavenworth is the home of the Tenth Cavalry. That's where they were sending us.

Q: Because it was all black?

A: Yeah. Well, except for officers. I didn't see any colored officers when I was down there.

Q: What did you end up doing?

A: They sent me to a unit that handled rations and supplies for troops in the combat zone. They called it "service and supply."

Q: Generally, what function did black troops serve?

A: Well, I went in the army in March 1942. We didn't see any Negroes in combat for a long time. I went to Africa and there were no Negro troops. Later they brought in an artillery company. Those were the first Negro combat troops we ran into. The bulk of the Negroes in Africa were in service and supply.

Q: When were you discharged?

A: I came home from France. I had been sent from Africa to Italy and then France. We were attached to the Third Army then.

Q: And this was still a segregated unit in service and supply?

A: Oh, very much so.

Boyd Wright, in 1944

Jimmy Bell, at far right above, was drafted into the army on October 13, 1941. He was sent from Fort Snelling to Fort Wolter in Texas for basic training. Later, he was stationed in Arizona before being sent to fight in the South Pacific. The women were members of the Women's Auxiliary Army Corps. They were among the first women to enlist during World War II. Jimmy Bell returned to Minneapolis in 1944 and became known as James Lawson.

Marjorie B. Anderson

Marjorie Anderson described the home front in her interview. Her story is one that many people will recognize, but one that is often overlooked in histories of the war. Her oral history is important because it describes everyday events in the lives of ordinary people.

Q: *When did your husband enlist in the navy?*

A: *It was 1942. We were living in Minneapolis. He was working for the YMCA at the time. He* was sent first to Miami. Then to Rhode Island and then to Boston for special training. At the end of the year, he went back to Miami, and I moved there with our son. We came back to Minneapolis when he was sent overseas in 1943.

Q: *Where did you live with your son while your husband was overseas?*

A: *We lived in a duplex on 10th Avenue in Minneapolis. The rent was $50.00 a month. The* navy sent some of my husband's salary to me every month. I can't remember how much it was. Probably about a $100.00 a month.

Q: *Would you describe rationing during the war? How did it work?*

A: *Rationing started in 1943, I think. We picked up our stamps at the Ration Board each month. They called it the War Board, at first. Stamps were distributed according to the number of people*

Marjorie Anderson and her son lived alone in Minneapolis during most of World War II. Her husband, George, enlisted in the navy in 1942. They lived for awhile in Miami, Florida, before George was sent to the South Pacific.

in your family. The stamps were not a substitute for money. They were like coupons you traded in. They allowed you to buy your share of those products.

Meat, sugar, gasoline, and flour were all rationed. I didn't use much sugar, but some people bought 50-pound bags of sugar when they heard that rationing would begin. They were afraid of being without sugar for the rest of the war.

Q: Did people trade ration stamps? Were stamps sold illegally?

A: Some people traded. I don't remember people selling them, but it's possible that happened. My father had a job that required a lot of driving, so he received more gasoline stamps. That was common for people in essential occupations.

Q: Was there a shortage of food or other items?

A: Yes, practically everything.

Eggs—though we had more eggs than they did in England. They got just one egg per person a week. Coffee was in short supply and that was rationed, too. Some people dried out their coffee grounds and used them again. There was a shortage of women's nylon stockings. I remember when Dayton's announced that they had a new shipment. Women lined up outside the building before the store opened. The line went around the block.

Q: Was it difficult to make ends meet on a salary from the navy?

A: There wasn't much money. I watched every nickel. All the rents were frozen, though. Landlords couldn't raise your rent. Most of us had Victory Gardens, you know. That helped. But there were just two of us and I didn't have much trouble getting by.

Marjorie Anderson, at left with her son at a Minneapolis park in 1943. The women above worked at a government office where people applied for ration stamps.

During the war, many people in the United States were suspicious of Japanese Americans. Some thought they might sabotage the United States. Others believed the Japanese Americans were in danger, threatened by people who blamed them for the war. The president of the United States issued an order requiring many Japanese Americans sent to camps where they would be guarded by the army until the war was over.

Joyce Yamamoto was born in one of the detention camps. Her interview describes the experience of Japanese Americans sent to the camps. The conversation begins with several open-ended questions. They give Yamamoto a chance to tell as much as she can remember about the topic. Open-ended questions do not ask for a "yes" or "no" answer. They usually result in longer, more informative answers. Here are some examples:

Q: *Joyce, you said you were born in a detention camp for Japanese Americans. Where was the camp and how was your mother sent there?*

A: *The story goes back to December 1941. My parents were living in California. My father owned a poultry business. My mother lived with his family while he traveled. In January 1942, he left California for Minnesota. While he was gone, the president issued his order. People were*

Joyce Yamamoto is a businesswoman who helps others start their own companies. She is an artist who makes beautiful pottery and paper. She is a teacher of economics, politics, and art. She is an activist who helped organize the National Association of Women Business Owners in Minnesota.

Joyce tells interesting stories about traveling to Japan. "I visited Japanese artists and businesses and a village that is a National Living Treasure."

In 1985, Joyce, who is also the mother of three children, was chosen for an award honoring women in the arts. She lives in St. Paul.

told they would have to leave their homes.

My mother went to stay with her parents. My grandfather Morishita owned a boardinghouse. A crew of fieldworkers stayed at the boardinghouse. My grandmother cooked for them and washed their clothes.

My grandfather was worried that he would be sent to one of the camps. One day he went to work and didn't come back. They took him to a camp in North or South Dakota. Soon my grandmother learned she and her children would be sent to a detention camp. There were six children in the family. My mother was the second oldest. She was 23. They could pack up only what they could carry with them. One of the hardest things for them was to sell their car. It was almost new, and they had paid $1,200.00 for it. In the days before they left, they had to sell it for just $25.00.

They were taken first to a racetrack. They arrived January 19, 1942. They were assigned to horse stalls or tents out on the track. They stayed there for about a month. Then they were taken on trains to an abandoned army camp near Rivers, Arizona. It was a pretty desolate spot. I believe the camp housed 3,000 people. They lived in old army huts. Each person was given a certain amount of space, hardly enough for a bed.

I was born on September 30, 1942. My mother says that she was fairly healthy when I was born. There were a lot of women with babies in the camps who, because of stress and not enough liquids, didn't have enough breast milk. So she breast-fed both me and another baby.

This group of men enlisted in the army on December 7, 1945. It was the fourth anniversary of the Pearl Harbor bombing. Their faces show this was a serious event.

197

Q: How about your father? How did he avoid being sent to a detention camp?

A: My father was working near Paynesville, Minnesota. He was not required to move into a camp because he was living away from the coast. He knew what was happening, but he could do nothing. He began checking and found that he could get us released if three upstanding citizens in town would sign an agreement to sponsor his family. He went to three people with whom he was friends. One of them refused to sign the papers. He finally completed all the requirements in February 1943. My mother and I were allowed to leave the camp and meet him in Paynesville. My grandparents stayed in the camp until 1946.

Q: Were most of the people in camp women, children, and older people?

A: Yes. All of the young men who were able immediately signed up for the army. They had a peculiar pride about defending the United States. When those young men came to visit their families, they had to visit them in the concentration camps.

Q: Would you describe conditions in camp?

A: The camp was organized by the army. They recruited Japanese Americans to help so it would

Japanese-American teachers and translators worked at the Japanese language school at Fort Snelling, October 19, 1945.

look more like self-rule. Both Japanese and English were spoken. People who had been teachers were allowed to teach children. I'm quite sure my uncles and aunts got most of their high school education in the camp.

There was rationing. People were limited to a half-pint of milk a day. They had gardens to help with the food supply. One of my aunts got tuberculosis and others did too. From my mother's point of view and mine, we were prisoners of war. There were guards on duty all of the time. There were rules about who could come in and who could go out and for what reason. We were under guard. We were given food every day, so it wasn't like the concentration camps you hear about in Germany. But detention was hard. So was the fact that everything had been taken from you. My grandfather could never get over the fact that the government would imprison citizens. When he got to the camp he expected to see his wife. But he was shocked that his kids were there. He never got over that.

Your grandparents and their parents may remember waiting in line at grocery stores, department stores, and gas stations during World War II. Ask them about shortages of food, appliances, and clothing. They may have saved photographs or ration stamps in family scrapbooks.

Your Own Oral History Project

Oral histories have become popular since cassette recorders have made research easier. Some oral history projects collect hundreds of interviews. Others may involve a student collecting one or two interviews for a class assignment. You and your class can start an oral history library with recorded interviews about events that people still remember.

Good oral history depends on planning and preparation. You need a cassette recorder, an extension cord, extra batteries, a microphone, a notebook and pencil, and several tapes. Use good equipment. (Poor equipment produces poor-quality recordings.)

Make sure you are clear about what you want to learn from the interview. Prepare some questions ahead of time. Begin with questions about a familiar or gen-

Wars always require sacrifice. The effect on personal lives is often cruel. This patriotic poster and photo of a young man in his victory garden are evidence of how Americans were affected by World War II.

eral topic. Listen closely for a chance to ask follow-up questions. Ask for details.

Find a quiet place for the interview. Put your microphone close to the person speaking. Test your machine and tape before the interview. Be sure everything is working properly.

Begin every interview with an introduction. Record information about the date, place, the people, and the topic involved in the interview. Ask your subject to sign a form giving you permission to use the material. Label the tape when you finish. Include the name of the person interviewed, the date, length of the interview, and your name.

Eventually, you will need a place to store your recorded tapes and a way to keep track of them, too. You may want to establish an oral history library with files for photographs, transcripts, and notes.

Recording an oral history is more than the pleasure of a conversation about the past. It is also a serious responsibility. Collecting good oral history is like discovering a primary source that has never before been studied. Your work can add to our knowledge and understanding of the past. It may be the best evidence we have of what people felt about the events of their lives.

The U.S. government asked everyone—even soldiers—to buy war bonds. The money was used like a loan to the government. Jimmy Bell, of Minneapolis, center, was stationed at Fort Huachuca in Arizona when he posed for this picture used to encourage others to buy bonds.

Activity 20
Sticking to Business

Five thousand hockey fans stood and cheered. Flags waved. A band played. The noise filled Blyth Arena at Squaw Valley, California. It was Sunday morning, February 28, 1960. The undefeated U.S. Olympic hockey team trailed Czechoslovakia 4 to 3 after two periods. Czech and American players skated around the rink waiting for the final period to begin.

The U.S. team had struggled through the first two periods. The Czechs scored after just eight seconds of play. The Americans managed to tie the score 3 to 3 by the end of the first period. The Czechs scored again early in the second and held on to the lead.

A referee blew his whistle. The U.S. players skated to their bench, huddled around their coach, and yelled encouragement to each other. The game began again. The crowd cheered louder. In a blur of color and noise, the players skated up and down the rink.

Suddenly, the puck bounced off the boards toward an American player, Billy Christian of Warroad, Minnesota. He skated toward the Czech goal, then passed to his brother, Roger. The American skater didn't hesitate. He shot the puck over the goalie's shoulder, high into the upper right-hand corner of the net. The game was tied. The crowd stood and cheered. Fifteen minutes remained in the game.

It wasn't yet ten o'clock Sunday morning. The Americans were playing their third game in four days. Thursday night they had upset the favored Canadians, 2 to 1. Only hours before, on Saturday night, they had beat the Soviet team, 4 to 3. It was the first time an American hockey team had ever beaten the Soviets. Billy Christian, now with his arms raised and cheering his brother's goal, had scored twice against them—once to tie and once to win.

Roger's goal inspired his teammates. Two minutes later they scored again to go ahead of the Czechs, 5-4. They scored again, and again, and again, and again! Each time the crowd cheered

wildly. A buzzer pierced the noise to end the game. The players threw their sticks into the air in exhausted celebration. Players on the bench climbed over the boards and skated to their teammates. They hugged each other and fell into a pile on the ice. They stood, lined up, and shook hands with their opponents. They skated around the rink again, then headed for the locker room. They had beaten the Germans and the Austrians. They upset the Canadians, the Soviets and the Czechs. They were Olympic champions, gold medal winners.

Hockey puts excitement in winter for many Minnesotans. Each game is an important event for players. The action is thrilling for fans. Little kids and big ones skate together in games on playground rinks. Rivalries between teams like the U of M Gophers and the UMD Bulldogs always attract a crowd. Hockey in Minnesota is also big business.

Olympic Gold Leads to a Good Idea

Here's a question about Minnesota history: What do Roger and Billy Christian have in common with Nellie Stone Johnson and Leeann Chin?

Here are some clues: Nellie Stone Johnson grew up on her family's farm in Dakota County. She moved to Minneapolis when she was 17 to find a job. She joined a labor union and fought for the rights of workers. Later, she started her own business, Nellie's Zipper and Shirt Repair.

Leeann Chin moved from China to Minnesota with her family in 1955. She worked at home to raise her family and at a job to earn money. In 1980 she started her own restaurant. By 1986 she owned and operated five restaurants in Minneapolis and St. Paul.

Roger and Billy Christian grew up in Warroad, near the Canadian border. After the 1960 Olympics they returned to live and work in their hometown.

Do those clues help you? If not, here's the answer: Johnson, Chin, and the Christian brothers are all Minnesota business owners. Their companies have been successful and are well known around the United States.

There's nothing new about doing business in Minnesota. In 1952, there were 83,583 companies in Minnesota. By 1980, the number had grown to 217,206. In 1988, 295,419 companies were owned and operated in Minnesota.

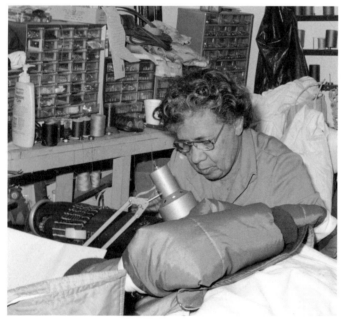

What do Nellie Stone Johnson, above, and Leeann Chin, at right, have in common with a couple of Olympic hockey players?

About 12,100 companies are started every year in the state.

Some businesses sell products like groceries, cars, clothing, or livestock and grain. Others sell services like health care, transportation, advertising, or snowplowing. Some businesses—like gas stations, restaurants, and newspapers—sell both a product and a service.

Businesses are organized to buy and sell things. Their purpose is to earn a profit for their owners. In this country, most businesses are owned by individuals. They may organize themselves as a company, corporation, partnership, or association, depending on how people share in making decisions. Some of the businesses organized each year in Minnesota will be successful. Others will fail. Some will stay in business for generations, others for only a short time.

All business owners have something in common. They each take a risk to get started in business. They bet their money and their time on the belief they can succeed. They each think they have the skill to produce something that others will buy. Each is willing to work hard.

Roger Christian

Billy Christian in his office at Christian Brothers, Inc.

Playground hockey, about 1940

205

An Idea Becomes Serious Business

Here's another question: What do Aaron Rutzick, Bill Robbins, and Shana Lohse have in common?

Their picture will give you a clue. Each of these high school hockey players is a customer of Christian Brothers, Inc., of Warroad. That's the company Roger and Billy Christian started with their brother-in-law, Hal Bakke, in 1964.

Christian Brothers, Inc., makes hockey sticks. It buys wood and other materials from businesses in New York, Pennsylvania, Wisconsin, Minnesota, and Canada. It hires employees. It pays for tools, heat and light, a factory and warehouse buildings, the cars and trucks it uses, its office supplies and equipment. It also pays taxes—for its share of the services provided by government.

The company pays all of those bills with money from sales of its

hockey sticks. It needs thousands of customers like Aaron, Shana, and Bill.

Christian Brothers, Inc., was Hal Bakke's idea. "Why not go into business for ourselves," he said. "Why not make hockey sticks? People still remember the Olympics and the hockey gold medal. The Christian brothers' name would help sell sporting goods."

Roger, Billy and Hal talked about the idea. It seemed like a

Members of the Central-Highland high school team are Shana Lohse, Aaron Rutzick, Jeff Robertson, Stig Sandell, Bill Robbins, and Pay Meyer. At right are Billy Christian and Hal Bakke, with sticks made in 1967.

good one. The *competition* was limited. Only one other company in the United States made hockey sticks. Roger and Billy were carpenters. They had the *skills* to do the work. Hal had *experience* running the business of a radio station in northern Minnesota. The *market* for hockey sticks was growing. Hockey was becoming more popular every year.

They decided to take the risk. They rented space in a Dairy Queen building. They bought wood, glue, paint, some new tools and equipment, and office supplies. They needed $1,000.00. They spent their own money and borrowed the rest.

In April 1964, they officially started business. Hal was the president, Billy Christian was vice-president, and Roger Christian treasurer. They called the company Christian Brothers, Incorporated. Its motto was "Hockey sticks made by hockey players."

The company began making and selling sticks. Roger, Billy, and Hal worked in the shop part time while they kept their full-time jobs. It was hard work and business was slow. During the first five years, the company earned only $21,000.00 more than it spent.

Each year Roger, Billy, and Hal learned more about the business. They learned to build better sticks for less money than the competi-

Roger, Hal, and Billy worked hard to start their business. They rented space for their first factory in an unused building. This photograph recorded the day when they were ready to ship their first sticks.

207

tion. More customers wanted to buy Christian Brothers sticks.

In 1969, they decided to expand the company—to work full time on hockey sticks, buy more equipment, hire more help, and build a factory. That was a big decision. They knew it was a risk. They would need more money for the business.

Like many companies, Christian Brothers did two things to raise the money: It borrowed money from people who charged interest and expected to be paid back. It also sold stock to people who were willing to become part owners. A *share of stock* represents a piece of ownership in a company. *Stockholders* share the profits when a company earns money. They also share the risk of losing money.

People in Warroad supported the company. The bank took the risk of lending money to Christian Brothers, Inc. Many of the people in town bought stock in the company.

The risk paid off. Christian Brothers sticks became more popular. They were sold in sporting goods stores in Minnesota and in other states where hockey was played. Professional players began using Christian Brothers sticks. So did college and high school players. So did children just learning to play hockey. Teams in Europe ordered Christian Brothers sticks.

Hockey was growing. Christian Brothers, Inc., grew, too. Profits grew and so did the competition. More companies in Canada and the United States began making hockey sticks. Each thought it could make a better stick, sell its product, and earn a profit.

Building hockey sticks depends on labor, investment, and technology. Follow each step of the process in the photographs on the next four pages. Begin with the one above: Hal Bakke, Lou Nanne of the North Stars, Roger Christian, and Stan Makita of the Chicago Blackhawks watch the new Christian Brothers factory being built.

Hockey Sticks Are Big Business

Hockey sticks have changed since Roger and Billy played in the Olympics. Billy scored twice against the Soviets with a Northland Pro. Roger used a Pro to score four times against the Czechs. In those days, almost every Minnesota hockey player used a Northland stick. The Pro model cost $2.50 in 1960. The stick was made entirely of ash. The blade was as straight as a ruler.

Competition, technology, and demand have changed that. The sticks are made from different materials now—fiberglass, aluminum, and several kinds of wood. The blades are curved. The shafts are painted with bright colors. The sticks are stronger and lighter than they used to be.

The lumber for Christian Brothers sticks is delivered to the factory already cut into shafts and blades. Stacks of each are set up at different places along a production line.

The long shaft is made of ash or sometimes a combination of maple, poplar, birch, and ash. Each shaft is tested and graded for strength and stiffness, then sanded smooth. Two small pieces of ash, each about three inches long, are glued to one end of the shaft. They help hold the blade in place. A groove is cut at that end of the shaft for the blade.

The blade is made from a piece of elm. It is cut to size and glued to the shaft.

The Christian Brothers factory makes more than 2,000 models and styles of hockey sticks. Each model uses different combinations of wood, fiberglass, and aluminum. Players of every age and skill test the new models before they are made on the production line.

Each step in the process adds to the cost of a stick. Why do you think so much work is done by hand?

Next, the edges and corners are sanded. The stick begins to take shape. The blade is heated in a bath of steam. Then it is placed between two rollers and bent to a slight curve. Some blades are curved more than others. Some are curved at the toe of the blade, others at the heel. Each hockey player has a favorite model. Christian Brothers makes more than 2,000 different styles to satisfy its customers.

At the next stop along the production line, someone wraps fiberglass over the blade of each stick. Then someone dips the blade into an epoxy solution that makes the fiberglass fabric stick to the blade. Some models are treated with fiberglass and epoxy along the shaft, too. The stick is set aside to dry for 48 hours.

The stick is sanded again. The shaft is painted and the name Christian USA is added. It's set to dry again.

In another part of the factory, men and women make sticks with aluminum shafts. Others work on goalie sticks with curved handles. Others work on new ideas that may improve the Christian Brothers sticks. "We get an idea and work on it for a while," said Billy. "When we think we have something, we go to a tool-and-diemaker and ask if he can build a machine according to our plans. I worked on ideas for our 2000 model for almost four years before we started making it in the factory."

The sticks are bundled and packed—two dozen to a box—and prepared for shipping. They are sent by truck and airplane to Japan, Canada, Italy, Germany, the Soviet Union, Sweden, and to cities in the United States.

There are nearly 20 companies making and selling hockey sticks now. They compete with each other for sales all over the world. Some of them make only hockey sticks. Others diversify—making other products, too. When the demand for hockey sticks grows, companies like Christian Brothers may make more sticks and earn more money. When the demand shrinks, those companies may earn less—or even lose money.

Christian Brothers, Inc., has grown. In 1982, it sold $2,500,000.00 worth of hockey sticks. In 1988, its sales grew to $3,500,000.00. The factory is busy all year.

There are at least seven reasons for Christian Brothers, Inc., success.
1. It chose to make and sell a product people wanted.
2. It had the skills and experience to produce the product.
3. It started slowly and borrowed money only when necessary.
4. It changed the product to satisfy its customers when technology made that possible.
5. Its sticks are among the best in the world, and they cost no more than the competition's.
6. The owners have made good decisions for the company.
7. It has good employees and the support of the hometown.

Rick Christian inspects sticks before they are packed for shipping.

Business Is Good History

Every business has a history. Some are stories of success, others are of failure. Some businesses grow to employ hundreds of people. Others remain the work of only a few individuals. Few begin with the excitement of an Olympic gold medal, but each has a special story to tell. Business history is about economics, politics, technology, and people.

Find a business that interests you in your neighborhood or town. Learn what product or service it sells. Find out who owns the company and how long it has been in business. Search for primary and secondary sources to learn more about the company. Examine its product and see how it has changed over the years. Record an oral history with the company owner or its employees. Study its technology. Compare its history with Christian Brothers, Inc. Find answers to these questions:

1. How did it begin?
2. What skills and experience did the owners have?
3. Did the owners borrow money or sell stock to get started?
4. How has the company changed?
5. What is its competition?
6. What effect has competition, technology, and demand had on the company and its product or service?

When you have the answers to those questions, write your own history of the business. Tell why you think it has been successful or

Can you figure out when this picture was taken? What evidence gives you a clue? What evidence in this story about the Christian Brothers business helps you pick a date for the photograph?

why it has had problems. Add drawings to your history. Include a picture of the product. Describe the technology used to make its product or deliver its service. Use a map to show its location or where the product is sold. When you finish, your history will tell about the lives of men and women who took a risk to start in business. It will also tell about the employees who have made history with their hard work.

This women's hockey team played in a Minneapolis league during the 1920s. Women's hockey is becoming popular again. Some area hockey associations have teams for girls. Some colleges have organized women's hockey teams with their own schedule of league games and tournaments.

There have been changes in hockey equipment since this picture was taken in Hibbing about 1948. How was equipment made differently then?

Illustration Credits

All images reproduced in the book that are not listed here or identified as to source are owned by the Minnesota Historical Society. The names of artists are omitted here when they have been included in captions. Photographers are listed when known.

Cover: *The Reapers* by Ogden M. Pleissner, The Minneapolis Institute of Arts.

Table of Contents: Unit II Detail of Winter Count courtesy of the State Historical Society of North Dakota. Unit III Detail of Traverse des Sioux by Francis D. Millet. Unit IV Photo from the Immigration History Reseach Center, Minneapolis. Unit VI Photo by Stephen Sandell.

Maps: viii Map by S. Augustus Mitchell Jr. ix Landsat imagery by National Air Survey Center, Blandensburg, Maryland.

Activity 1: 10, 11, 12, 13 Drawings from *On the Banks of Plum Creek* by Laura Ingalls Wilder, illustrations by Garth Williams, pictures copyright 1953 by Garth Williams, copyright © renewed 1981 by Garth Williams. 12 "Illustrating the Little House Books" by Garth Williams from *The Horn Book Magazine*, December 1953, p. 413, reprinted by permission of The Horn Book, Inc. 13 Photo courtesy of The Laura Ingalls Wilder Home and Museum, Irene Lichty Collection.

Activity 2: 18, 24 Maps courtesy of Sanborn Map Company, Inc., 629 Fifth Avenue, Pelham, New York 10803. For additional maps, contact Sanborn Map Company. 19 Dakota maps from Smithsonian Institution, Bureau of American Ethnology Publications, American Ethnology Report, Vol. 10, 1889. 22 Bess Wilson portrait, University of Minnesota's Photographic Laboratories.

Activity 3: 33 Map by Patricia Isaacs.

Activity 4: 37 Town of Currie, 38 Currie courthouse, 39 Currie depot, 41 Silvernale family, and 43 Currie family courtesy of Louise Gervais, End-O-Line Museum, Currie, Minnesota.

Activity 5: 44 Photo courtesy of the State Historical Society of North Dakota. 46 Portrait of Nodinens and 48 Portrait of Swift Dog by permission of the Smithsonian Institution Press from the Bureau of American Ethnology Publications, catalogue no. 522, Smithsonian Institution, Washington, D.C., photo no. 75-7766 and photo no. 3360-A. 49, 50 Details from Winter Count courtesy of the State Historical Society of North Dakota. 51 Illustrations from *The Jeffers Petroglyphs Site*, Minnesota Historical Society Press.

Activity 6: 52 Photo by Douglas A. Birk, The Institute for Minnesota Archaeology, Inc. 55, 57, 59, 60, 61 Photos from The Institute for Minnesota Archaeology, Inc. 58 Site drawing by Stephen Sandell from map by Douglas A. Birk. 58, 59 Drawings by Douglas A. Birk.

Activity 7: 62 National Archives of Canada, Ottawa, negative no. C-2774. 64 From *A Toast to the Fur Trade*, Robert C. Wheeler, copyright 1985, artwork by David Christofferson, courtesy of Wheeler Productions, St. Paul. 68 Map by Patricia Isaacs. 69 Trading post illustration courtesy of National Archives of Canada, Ottawa. Painting, *The Portage* by William Armstrong.

Activity 8: 73 Drawings by Rhoda R. Gilman. 74, 75 Map by Patricia Isaacs. 77 Drawing by Samuel Seymour, engraved by J. Hill for publication in *Narrative* published in 1924. 78 Map by Patricia Isaacs. 79 Drawing of Milwaukee by George J. Robertson, courtesy of State Historical Society of Wisconsin, Madison, Wisconsin. Photo of locomotive courtesy of Association of American Railroads. 80 Great Lakes ship, *Princeton*, Dossin Great Lakes Museum, Detroit, Michigan.

Activity 9: 82 Lithograph by Albert Ruger. 83 Map by Patricia Isaacs. 86 Photo of John McKusick courtesy of Washington County Historical Society.

Activity 10: 94 Map from *Mitchell's School and Family Geography*, 1856.

Activity 11: 111 Camp Traverse des Sioux, 112 Dakota Girl, 112 Two Dakota Men, 113 Dakota Evening Meal, 114 Sleepy Eye, and 115 Little Crow by Frank B. Mayer, photos courtesy of Edward E. Ayer Collection, The Newberry Library, Chicago, Illinois.

Activity 12: 124 Charts prepared by Janet Christensen. 126 Photo by Hoard and Tenney, Winona. 127 Map from *Andreas Atlas*, 1874.

Activity 13: 130 Photo by Moses C. Tuttle, St. Paul. 131 Oliver Evans's steam engine from *Niles' Weekly Register*, vol. 3, 1813.

Activity 14: 136 Coloration by Earl Gutnik. 140, 141 Photos from Immigration History Research Center, Minneapolis.

Activity 15: 147 Photo of Eugene Debs from Eugene V. Debs Foundation, Terre Haute, Indiana. 149 Photo of Eugene Debs courtesy of Cunningham Memorial Library, Indiana State University, Terre Haute, Indiana. 153 Photo from *St. Paul Daily News*.

Activity 17: 166 Game board, 168 Drawings, 177 Artwork courtesy of Children's Literature Research Collection, Walter Library, University of Minnesota. 170 Photo by Randolph R. Johnston, St. Paul. 171 Photo of F. Scott Fitzgerald courtesy of Princeton University Library. 173, 175 Photos courtesy of Gordon Parks. 176 Photo courtesy of Elizabeth B. Larsen. 177 Drawing by Stephen Sandell.

Activity 18: 178, 180, 181, 182 Photos of Alice Nelson by Stephen Sandell. 179 Photo of women quilting from George Luxton Collection, MHS. 183 Photo of quilt by Eric Mortenson. 185 Photos courtesy of Corrine Pearson, owner of Hmong Handwork, St. Paul, Minnesota. 187 Photo courtesy of State Historical Society of North Dakota.

Activity 19: 190, 191 Photos courtesy of Northwestern Minnesota History Center, Moorhead. 192, 193 snapshot, 201 courtesy of James Lawson. 193 Photo of Boyd Wright courtesy of Boyd A. Wright. 194, 195 Anderson photos courtesy of Marjorie Anderson. 196 Photo by Stephen Sandell.

Activity 20: 202 Photo by Jeff Christensen. 204 Leeann Chin photo courtesy of Leeann Chin, Inc. 205 Bill Christian, Roger Christian, 206 Hockey players, and 210, 211 Photos by Stephen Sandell. 206, 207, 208, 209 Photos courtesy of Christian Brothers, Inc. 212 Photo from *St. Paul Dispatch* and *St. Paul Pioneer Press*. 213 Hibbing hockey game photo by Al Heitman. Women's hockey team photo from the *Minneapolis Journal*.

Other Credits

Activity 5: 49 Swift Dog's music courtesy of Smithsonian Institution, Bureau of American Ethnology, Bulletin 61, 1918.

Activity 17: 174 Lyrics from "No Love" used by permission of Gordon Parks.